A QUIET DAWDLE AROUND THE ATLANTIC

THE BUILDING AND VOYAGING OF 'OSPRAY'
A COPY OF SLOCUM'S FAMOUS 'SPRAY'
BY JAMES F MELLOR

Grosvenor House
Publishing Limited

This book is published by
Grosvenor House Publishing Ltd
28-30 High Street, Guildford, Surrey, GU1 3EL.
www.grosvenorhousepublishing.co.uk

A CIP record for this book
is available from the British Library

ISBN 978-1-78148-810-2

Dedication

I wish to dedicate this book to my son Andrew, who flew out from Australia to join us in the Caribbean for part of the voyage. He later died in Australia.

I also dedicate the book to Geoff and Joyce Knibb, both of whom I have known since early childhood. Geoff and Joyce were cruelly parted by illness some time ago. Joyce died a few days after Geoff without knowing that he had slipped his cable. Some romantic souls suggested there might have been telepathic communication between the two. I can imagine Joyce faithful to the last saying, "Hey up, hang on, I'm coming too!" Geoff flew out to the Azores to sail with us back to Wales. Geoff was a man of few words but was renowned for having the driest of dry wits!

Acknowledgements

I wish to acknowledge my first wife Ruth for planting the acorn! Also to the sterling and enthusiastic help given to me, by my eldest son Robert, a thinking welder. Also for the help from my other two sons, Mark and Jonathan, which was much valued. And to all those who helped with the building and fitting out of *Ospray,* e.g. Chris Wotton and Paul Curley. Thanks to the Biker Reverend for blessing our boat prior to her departure for the coast. Thanks to Mary Palmer for typing my first articles. To my wife Else for her enthusiasm in all aspects of this book and especially the massive task of typing it up, usually several times! Thanks, Else, also for being my loyal First Mate in all respects of our voyage. Thanks to Stuart and Ann Reid for their diligent proof reading and for being excellent neighbours!

Many thanks to Practical Boat Owner and BWee Caribbean Beat magazines for their enthusiasm in the writing of this book.

PART 1

Chapter 1

Old Slocum's Boat in Steel

"How do you fancy building a boat to shunt ice?" I queried my eldest lad Rob. Rob wrenched his eyes from the writhings of Legs & Co. on the television and swivelled his tousled head in my direction to where I was ensconced by a roaring fire with a pile of boat plan catalogues.

"You mean old Slocum's Boat?"

"Yes", I said, "but in steel".

My first wife Ruth was a staff nurse at the local hospital and bought me a book from their autumn fair which had a bookstall. Joshua Slocum titled it 'Sailing Alone Around The World'. He was the first to accomplish this feat, which many said could not be achieved in 1895. They say that great oaks from little acorns grow; some acorn! Thanks Ruth! This great oak strangely grew into a steel boat, which we named *Ospray* after a visit from a holy man on a motorbike who having learned of our project came to offer his blessing. Knowing Latin and seeing the boat's frame in its skeletal form commented on the name *Ospray*, which he assumed, meant the "bones of the *Spray*". This tickled my fancy and so the name stuck. Having blessed the boat the Reverend revved up his bike and roared off up the lane.

Thus began a flame which burned steadily, occasionally ferociously until the vessel was complete and long afterwards. I was still in fulltime employment, so my evenings and weekends were occupied by countless hours of reading. One of my strong beliefs has always been to use many opinions rather than one, which I have found to give a broad and balanced opinion.

I was given great encouragement by the editor of the Practical Boat Owner, Denny Desouter, who was very enthusiastic about this article and suggested a series and the possibility of a book to follow.

Now Rob is a welder by trade and, like Barkis, he was willing.

The photograph in Bruce Roberts' catalogue of a rugged, powerful vessel of unmistakable fishing boat origins fanned a glowing enthusiasm into a flame.

Thus began the building of *The Ospray.* The realisation of a long cherished dream to build a vessel, which could be sailed into the waters off Greenland to explore the rich cod and halibut fishing. What vessel could be more appropriate that one whose ancestors were built to reap the harvests of the North Atlantic, albeit with nets rather than rod and line?

We decided at the outset to name our boat *The Ospray* in honour of Josh Slocum's famous vessel *The Spray* and to leave her in no doubt that she is expected to sniff out some good fishing in various parts of the world.

Being 40 feet long excluding bowsprit, with a beam of 14 ft 2in and displacing 16 tons, she has a great capacity for stores, a coal stove and a thumping big diesel engine – I am no purist!

The plans were ordered and arrived within days. I was filled with apprehension. The mass of detail was daunting. Being no craftsman would I be up to the job? Would Rob, being a lad of 20 summers be constantly lured away by the local lasses – or the lads at the pub?

I needn't have worried. We quickly realised that in order to avoid conflict we needed to establish a regular routine. We agreed to work weekends and three evenings per week.

Although this schedule has been kept up – apart from holidays and special circumstances – we have adopted an easy going approach which has made the project a labour of love, with plenty of coffee breaks to discuss the next move though we didn't have Slocum's enviable distraction of old whaling captains who would 'work along up' to the yard and 'gam' with him whilst he rested on his adze.

After 9 months of weekend and evening work the hull was welded up and ready for grit-blasting.

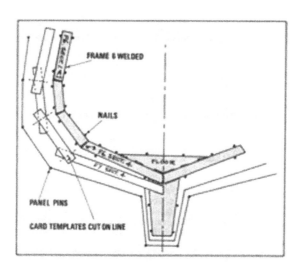

We transferred the shapes of the frames to builder's ply, cut card templates for them and held them in position with nails during welding.

Now some nine months or 821 man-hours later the hull is complete and ready for grit blasting. With her clipper bow she looks quite beautiful. But then parents are noted for perceiving beauty in their offspring.

To anyone teetering on the brink I would say jump in with both feet. You will wish you had done it years ago!

COST TO DATE	£
Plans	374
Steel, including steel for	
Decks and superstructure	2060
Angle grinder (9 inch)	96
Gas cutting equipment	98
Acetylene and oxygen to date	86
Hire of MIG welder for welding	
Seams, including wire and argon	212
Welding rods	38
Protective clothing, two sets	46
Sundries, small tools, etc.	49
	3285

Whilst awaiting the arrival of the steel and accumulating the necessary equipment, Rob and I poured over the plans and read everything we could find on steel boat building, including all our old PBOs for eight years and Mike Pratt's excellent book *Own a Steel Boat* and Ian Nicholson's *Small Steel Craft*. I would strongly recommend this course of action as it provides a cross section of opinion on various aspects of boat building in steel. During the course of the project one acquires a feel for the job and forms one's own ideas but at first it is comforting to be able to hold the hand of someone who has done it before.

Even so I feel that having completed the hull and with the great wisdom of hindsight we have identified and overcome sufficient hidden pitfalls and evolved easier ways of doing things to be able to build a second hull in less than half the time. Often, after sweating and struggling with a job for hours or even weeks an easy or more accurate solution presents itself.

It is with this in mind that I put pen to paper. Not as an instruction on how to build steel boats – after all one hull doesn't make an expert – but in the hope that some of our ideas, often discovered towards the end of a job, may save other amateurs the trouble of finding out for themselves.

Amateurs have one advantage over professionals; they have no tramlines of tradition to run along and by approaching a problem from a completely fresh angle, many unorthodox but effective techniques are developed.

Our cutting and grinding bench in use. A wooden wedge under the lever gives variable clamping pressure.

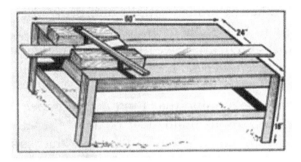

Our cutting and grinding bench in use. A wooden wedge under the lever gives variable clamping pressure.

After spending slow long hours cutting with the grinder we opted to flame-cut our metal. Heat distortion was negligible.

SETTING OUT AND MAKING THE FRAMES

The plans from Bruce Roberts and some other designers come with full size paper patterns showing the frames in half-section. These are laid out edge-to-edge and matched up like wallpaper so that the lines may be transferred to more durable material. The instructions were to make the frames in two halves then weld together. However herein lies the first pitfall for the unwary. Making things in halves, as any engineer will tell you – usually after you have done the job – ain't easy.

Rob and I had made seven frames in halves that matched perfectly. Smugly we welded them to the floors, also cut in halves from ¼ inch plate. The two halves were welded carefully together. Later we were stunned to find that the total widths were out by as much as 1 ¼ inches!

Cause – magnification of tiny variation in welding gap over a few inches when multiplied by width of frame.

Result – two weeks painstakingly dismembering seven frames with angle grinder. Ugh!

Conclusion - if at all possible set out your frame patterns full size. We did this later and found the whole business easier and more accurate.

Our method, which worked well enough, was to line the workshop floor with ¾ inch shuttering ply obtained second hand from a building site, and painted white. Then lay out the frame patterns, match up carefully and join with masking tape. Next, the centre line and all the frames were marked by tapping panel pins through the plans into the ply after reinforcing the plan at each point with an inch of masking tape. We alternated copper plated pins with steel ones for alternate frames to avoid confusion. The plans were then lifted carefully off and flopped over to create a mirror image using the centre line as a hinge point. This latter part was done after the disaster with the first seven frames.

CUTTING THE FRAMES

Before you start cutting metal invest in some decent protective gear. I thought once that steel was a cold material in which to work. However there is nothing cool about a copious stream of sparks from the angle grinder flowing through a glowing hole in your upper trouser leg. Another thing I found distracting is the large globule of molten metal which, sporting a tail like Hayley's Comet flies unerringly through one of your lace holes!

Even when this happened to Rob rather than myself I found his howls of anguish spoilt my concentration and one can easily spoil a perfectly good piece of metal. I know of one boat builder who resorted to wearing Wellingtons as they have no lace holes, until one day a short piece of red hot frame bar dropped down his right wellie to lodge firmly against his instep. The poor lad took off around the workshop issuing forth billows of smoke and loud screams. His partner when pressed for an explanation as to why the lad's boot was not cut away retorted, "I would have but I couldn't catch him!"

So buy a good long leather apron, stout leather boots with gusseted tongue, leather gauntlets, eye shields and facemask. A beret is a good idea as it deflects those large sparks which crackle through your hair to lie sizzling on the scalp whilst, with grim determination, you continue to cut your straight line, trying to ignore the pain until the spark goes out.

It was not until the grinding off of the final welds that I discovered the comfort of earmuffs against the penetrating screech of the angle grinder.

Initially we began marking off the sections of frame to be cut by measuring the length and angles on the plan with a steel tape and protractor. This was laborious, time consuming and liable to error. After doing several frames in this tedious fashion we developed a method, which was far quicker, easier and foolproof. The frames on *The Spray* are

2 ½ inches wide so using a Stanley knife we cut numerous strips of this width from thin card. The strips of card where then placed on the frame patterns and cut off with the Stanley knife at their intersection with each other, which automatically bisects the angle as required. Like the safety pin, this system seems obvious when you think about it but was evolved only after persuading son No. 3, Mark, to bisect numerous angles with a pair of compasses. Sorry about that lad. Still you'll never forget how to bisect angles again!

Each card template was then marked as in the diagram. No measuring is involved. When cutting begins the template is placed on the frame bar and cut off lines marked with a felt tipped pen. The beauty of this system is that production line methods may be used to cut off a few dozen sections at a time without traipsing back and forth across the pattern floor measuring and re-measuring. Now was it 13 $^{15}/_{16}$ or 15 $^{13}/_{16}$? Furthermore each section can be checked against its template for accuracy.

Having read of the horrors of distortion caused by gas cutting we cut over half the frames using a cutting disc in the angle grinder. This does leave a nice clean edge but cutting 2½ inch by $^{3}/_{8}$ inch bar 368 times is a longish job. Then one Sunday we ran out of cutting discs – which are expensive items at over £2 each – and decided to fly in the face of convention by using the acetylene torch with a fine nozzled step cutter. We were surprised to find that there was no measurable distortion and that the temperature rise 2 inches away from the cut was no more than with the much slower angle grinder. Since the cut edges have to be bevelled for welding the slightly cleaner edge left by the angle grinder is no advantage.

This is one of the few areas where I dissent from Mike Pratt's views. Sorry Mike! Perhaps the secret lies in the use of the single jet ASNM nozzle, which localises the heat input far more than the multi-jet type nozzle. The ASNM nozzle is recommended for plate up to 3mm thick but we have cut material up to 12mm thick with no difficulty, leaving a very clean edge. In fact we have cut out the entire hull with one nozzle.

The procedure we eventually evolved for the last few frames was briefly as follows:

1. Cut out card templates as described.
2. Using templates mark out and cut off frame sections.
3. Bevel all edges which are to be welded.
4. Cut out floors from ¼ inch plate.
5. Place floor and frame sections in place with nails to avoid movement during welding. Turn over and repeat.

Believe it or not, the making of the frames, including rectifying mistakes and an awful lot of pondering took us 246 man-hours. The last few frames averaged a shade over 3 hours each, which for 23 frames would be around 70 hours!

Ah! The wisdom of hindsight!

Chapter 2

Ospray's Bones Take Shape

'The Seasons came quickly while I worked. Hardly were the ribs of the sloop up before apple trees were in bloom'.

As it was with Slocum, so it was with us, but the easy way came only after the hard. Now setting up the frames on a steel hulled boat merits great care as on the fairness of the frames depends the appearance of the boat.

A skin of steel plate weighing several tons must be supported by the frames so the building jig must be rigid and strong. Since it is impossible to set up all frames accurately the first time, provision must be made for vertical, lateral and linear adjustment of each frame.

Rob and I elected to build our hull upside down for ease of plating and welding. We have had cause to be thankful that we adopted this alternative many times when gravity has been a welcome assistant whilst persuading some of the heavier plates into position.

Our jig was made from scrap materials except for the headstocks, which were cut from 2in x 2in angle bar, which will be used for bulkhead stiffeners and furniture framing at fitting-out time.

The frames were slung from a 3in diameter steel tube by butchers' type hooks made from $^5/_{16}$in diameter reinforcing bar, and long eye-bolts sold by agricultural suppliers for fence wire strainers. The vertical adjustment was accomplished by welding to each frame a drilled lug cut from angle bar. The eye-bolt was threaded through the lug and the position of the nut provides the height adjustment.

Lateral adjustment was accomplished by bolting the frame to the headstock by means of a two-inch slot cut in the headstock.

The frame may be moved forward or aft by sliding the butchers' hook along the steel tube.

When the frames are bolted to the headstock via the slots, the nuts should be left only hand tight. This allows them to be tapped into precise position with a hammer when fairing up with a fairing batten. The nuts are then tightened up hard.

The first few frames were heaved into position by muscle power. Their weight and awkward shape as they swung and clanged about, gave rise to speculation on such varied topics as the minimum number of fingers required to play the guitar and the current price of a surgical truss! However, necessity gave birth once more and a three-part tackle was devised which worked beautifully but looked so splendidly nautical that we should undoubtedly have used it even if it had been the most dismal failure.

With the frames set up and stringers welded in we could start plating up.

CUT ANOTHER NOTCH

Cutting the 138 notches in the frames to receive the ¾in round bar stringers was a job, which Rob and I contemplated with foreboding as a long and tedious task. In fact the job was completed quite easily in under four hours. A template was cut from a piece of frame bar, clamped in place with Mole grips and the notch was cut out with the torch.

The stringer bars were tack-welded into the notches after being persuaded into position with the sterling assistance of *James Crow Esq.* A creature of such astonishing versatility that, waiving all rights and charges, I reproduce his lines and dimensions in order, dear reader, that you may have one of your very own.

The 40-foot stringer bars – two 20-foot lengths butt-welded together – were draped around the chines and lashed roughly into position with baler twine. The crow was then used to lever them into exact position, leaving about $1/4$ in protruding from the notch so that the plate would butt onto the shoulder of the bar.

It is important to get this just right. Too much bar sticking out and the vile job of grinding off seems to take centuries; too little means large gaps to be filled with weld which is expensive and time consuming.

By now the piles of steel really began to take on the shape of a boat or, as one passer-by observed, the skeleton of a stranded whale.

"Whaling captains came from afar to survey it. When a whaling captain hove in sight I just rested on my adze awhile and 'gammed' with him". Slocum said it all, long ago...

On one day of torrential rain, Rob and I were standing by, brew in hand, gazing in rapturous astonishment at our handiwork when our local parson hove in sight, there being a desperate shortage of whaling captains in our vicinity.

This modern-day man of the cloth – "call me Vic" – with hair tumbling over reversed collar and clad in motor-bike boots, had heard of our project and had come to offer his blessing on the embryo ship. Rob and I were deeply touched.

"*Ah yes*", mused the Vic, "*Os-spray. Bones of the Spray.*" This natty play on words had escaped Rob and I but we were impressed. I remarked to our learned friend that if this rain kept up much longer perhaps he had better have a word with the gaffer to find out how much time we had to get the plates on whilst he sorted out some of the beasts into pairs, and to please remember that Jason and Janie, our two spaniels, had made a firm booking.

After a long look at our huge skeleton, crouched in the barn in the fading light, the Reverend revved up his machine and roared away, having promised to return at some later date when the plates were on in order to bless the progress.

Meanwhile, always looking ahead, Rob and I obtained our masts. The masts of *The Ospray* are to be grown sticks

Rob and plate 1. Building upside down lets gravity work for you and also simplifies welding.

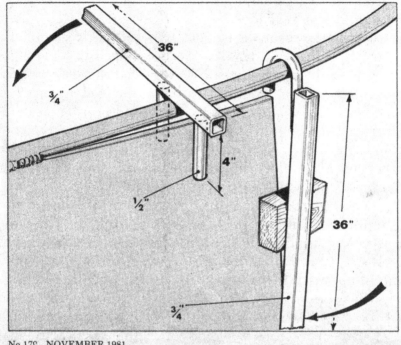

No 179 NOVEMBER 1981

of Sitka Spruce. This decision was made first because I am a bit of a traditionalist, and second on account of not being able to afford aluminium ones.

If I had imagined it was going to be as simple as that then I was in for one big surprise. That is the intrigue of boatbuilding. Each aspect is a study in itself. I spent countless hours of eager research in order that the wisest options were always taken.

On the subject of spars one writer was alarmingly fatalistic. It was, he stated, quite easy to tell a good mast from a bad mast because the good masts stayed up whilst the bad ones fell down. Rob and I are unanimous in our preference for vertical masts so we began to ask around.

It was too much to expect that Shrewsbury, in the heart of England, would be bursting at the seams with folk steeped in maritime maters. This is where a pub full of retired whaling captains would have come in dead handy. Lucky old Josh says I!

Norway Spruce and Douglas Fir were most commonly used but more recently, Sitka Spruce, which is some 17% lighter than Norway, seems to be regarded as the very finest mast material, so long as it can be obtained in the best quality or *'aeroplane grade'* used for load-bearing struts of aircraft. This should be slow grown in a close stand in cool conditions, which produces a strong straight stem with little taper and small knots. Sitka has, in any case, much less taper than Norway, which means less wood to remove.

Enquiries revealed that there was such a stand high up on a Welsh mountainside only 30 miles from home. For some reason or other the stand had not been thinned so the stems grew straight and tall. The day came when Rob and I set out to choose our masts in the vast forests surrounding Lake Vyrnwy.

The vista of nearly 20 million trees was breathtaking and we were soon striding through them with the forester who said that many forests would offer this facility to boat builders provided that he was willing to pay a little over commercial price for selected timber.

A quick walk through the Yellow Pages under *'Timber Merchants'* or *'Forestry'* should produce results. However, should you live in striking distance of Wales and the border countries, I can give you the names and telephone numbers of two people I have found helpful:

David Webster of Charles Ransford and Sons, is himself a boating enthusiast and always ready to talk timber.

This firm can supply various timbers including some English hardwoods. Particularly attractive, I think, is good quality Douglas Fir sawn to size for £2.80 per cubic foot. For 20p extra this can be partly kiln dried to below 26% moisture from which point it will dry readily, in a well-ventilated garage, to below 16% provided it is properly stacked with spaces between each plank.

Michael Duggleby of Severn Trent Water Authority's Lake Vyrnwy Estate is always eager to talk business and can supply timber, including Sitka Spruce, either in the round for spars or sawn to size.

We chose three trees for our two masts in case one proved to be unsuitable. The cost was £80 for three splendid masts. The trees were felled without delay and it was a great moment to see our mainmast crash to earth where it looked gigantic. Fate then played one of her better hands.

I discovered a timber merchant working in the area who agreed to haul my sticks home for £35. It also transpired that he had a redundant Ford diesel engine of 100bhp. Another £50 changed hands and the engine was mine.

Thus at one stroke did we acquire the basis of our two forms of motive power. I only wish it always happened that way!

Chapter 3

Using Gravity to Advantage

A great day in the building of a steel boat is when the first plate is welded into place.

The steel bones of our version of Slocum's famous vessel, *The Spray*, crouched in the barn like the skeleton of some giant marine armadillo without the armour. The forging of this armour was the next stage in the reincarnation of a vessel which, even at this stage, seemed to be surrounded by an aura of dormant power.

Rob and I elected to use 5mm mild steel plate for the hull except for the stern and keel, which are of 6mm thickness. Plate down to 3mm thickness may also be used for hull plating, although more care is then need to avoid flat spots between frames and distortion caused by welding. However this is not so great a problem now that MIG welding with its much lower heat input is more easily available.

I would strongly recommend the use of a MIG welder for the final welding of the seams and, I have regretted not having bought one in the first place rather than hire. The advantages are substantial.

In Metallic Inert Gas welding a continuous roll of wire is fed through a nozzle, through which is also blown a shroud on inert gas – an Argon mixture is best – which prevents the molten metal being oxidised by the air. This replaces the flux that surrounds a normal welding rod. It is this flux which forms the slag that requires to be chipped off the weld, often leaving pockets and rust traps. I am not altogether frantic about its tendency to lodge in one's ear whilst sizzling hot from the weld!

SPEED

MIG welding must be at least four times faster than stick welding as there is no rod changing and no slag to chip off or form rust traps. I believe MIG welding of steel boats is mandatory in some countries.

EASE OF USE

Although there is a certain knack to MIG welding, which must be acquired, it is certainly easier to use than a stick welder.

LESS DISTORTION

Heat is concentrated just where it is required which means longer runs are possible and in many cases continuous runs can be made rather than skip welding, which is essential with stick welding, to avoid distortion.

PREPARATION

Is less critical and gaps caused by poor fit are more tolerable and can be filled without risk of slag traps and weak welds.

VERSATILE

Positional welding is not so difficult with MIG welding.

Firms that sell or hire MIG equipment may be found in the Yellow Pages. One such firm is Shirehire, Cemetery Road, Telford, telephone Telford 502833, where Steve Woodhouse will be pleased to talk business and arrange for a demonstration. This firm often has second-hand units for sale from £300 upwards. Hire charges range from £25 per week for a single phase unit to £40 for a hefty 3 phase model capable of laying down several hundred pounds of weld in a

A 10lb weight was used to counterpoise the angle grinder. Full protective clothing including filter and goggles are essential for safe working.

week's work. Wire costs are around £10 for a 12-kilo drum and Argon mixture gas costs about £14 per cylinder.

Echoing Josh Slocum's sentiments: *"It was my purpose to make my vessel stout and strong"* – Looking now at my little ship I am pleased that we chose 5mm plate. A determined man with a sledgehammer would be hard put to make much impression. For that insidious enemy of steel boats, corrosion, there is a generous margin.

Steel plate is mighty stuff – an 8 ft x 4 ft sheet of 6mm plate weighs 270lbs and it quickly became apparent that we should need something on which to cart the stuff around. Our problem was soon solved by a visit to a local junkyard where a British Railways-type bogie became mine for £15. His has proved a real boon and we use it as a mobile bench for cutting, grinding, welding and a host of other jobs.

Boat builders, for your pocket's sake, acquaint yourself with your local scrap yards, seek them out and befriend their proprietors and great bargains will be yours!

One such treasury, deep in the heart of the Shropshire countryside, is the yard of R. S. Beaver & Son, who stock the most astonishing range of steel sections and second hand equipment, including sectional buildings big enough to build a big boat in. £1000 can easily be saved in this manner.

However, I digress, back to the job in hand, plating the vessel. For each steel plate a hardboard template was made. This did not work out as expensive as one might suppose as many of the templates were able to be used several times by cutting them down for smaller plates.

Marking out and cutting hardboard templates presents no great difficulty provided that certain pitfalls into which we initially fell are avoided.

Hardboard is easier to cut than steel so it pays to spend time making an accurate template. This saves time trimming off surplus steel or, later, filling in large gaps with weld, both of which we had to do on our earlier plates. Josh Slocum knew a thing or two when he said: *"the planking was tedious but afterwards the caulking was easy."*

MAKING UP VERY ACCURATE HARDBOARD TEMPLATES

The hardboard is held against the outside of the erected frames and made to conform to the curves of the hull, touching everywhere possible even if this means enlisting extra help. Don't imagine that you can *'roll'* the sheet round, marking as you go, this will lead to substantial errors. I know, I've tried doing it that way!

The template is then marked from the inside of the boat drawing along the chine bars. Each plate should end between frames and not on them. The template is cut out with a jigsaw and then offered up before being trimmed to exact size with a convex Surform plane.

The template is laid on the steel plate and, believe it or not, that hardboard may then be used as a profile to cut around with the torch using the single-jet ASNM nozzle. I have not heard of this method being used elsewhere. The hardboard does not, as I should have imagined, immediately burst into flames although it does char a little round the edges.

The burnt edge of the plate must then be dressed with the angle grinder and given a bevel of about 60 degrees so that the weld will penetrate through the gap, which should be about half the plate thickness.

Now comes the exciting moment when the first plate is ready to be lifted into place and tack-welded. There are several ways of doing this. Naturally Rob and I, for the first ten plates or so, chose the most obvious but dangerous method of all. The plates were heaved up the side of the hull by muscle power and joggled into position amidst hideous screams whilst fingernails fell like autumn leaves!

How curious a phenomenon it is that the length of time required to strike up an arc is directly proportional to the degree of discomfort suffered by the person who with streaming brow and bulging eyes strains the plate into position whilst the welder splutters and fizzles. Of course the more intelligent of you will probably do initially what we did eventually; build a gantry from which to lift your plates.

The whole job suddenly became safer, easier, much quicker and far less exhausting. A little time spent in preparation pays off handsomely.

Our gantry was a 3in tube slung over the ship from which we hung our tackles. Do not be reluctant, as we were, to mar your nice smooth plates by welding on lifting eyes. These knock off easily and 5 seconds work with a grinder removes all trace.

Having, by your chosen method, raised the plate into position, taking a touch off here and there with the grinder to ensure a snug fit and correct welding gap, the plate, said the book, is tacked into position. What a delightful impression of nonchalance is conjured up by the phrase 'tacked into position'. Far from the expletives hissed through gritted teeth whilst persuading those plates into their proper curves. Even with the most devilishly clever application of double levers some plates with a powerful curve will severely tax your strength and vocabulary.

I remember one of our bow plates on which I had spent over an hour heaving and straining into position. Suddenly

Once we saw the value of them we welded on lugs with gay abandon – they can be quickly knocked off and the tack welds ground clean. They certainly made levering plates into place much easier.

the lever slipped. With a deafening clang, which frightened the living daylights out of me, the plate straightened out – peeling off a row of tack welds like the press-studs on a girl's blouse.

Again I suggest you do initially what we did eventually. Weld lugs on freely and with abandon. Right from the start. Not after struggling for half an hour.

Plating a boat is hard work. There are, however, few activities that are its equal for smug satisfaction. I have often stood in the gloaming after the day's toil, gazing at the three or four plates, each with its own sweet curve, past, which I would imagine, the green ocean water gliding.

The day the final plate went on my elation knew no bounds. It was rumoured that the months of hyperactivity had rendered me two pence short of a shilling.

However until then my greatest claim to fame in the field of construction had been the building of a rather ugly stone fireplace. So I forgive myself for feeling smug. For reasons described earlier the final welding of the seams is best done with a MIG welder. Much longer runs can be made without risk of distortion but this must not be ignored and there should be a balance of welding on each side the ship.

The next job is vile. It is monotonous, dirty, noisy and endless. The grinding off of the welded seams to leave a

Ospray *wearing her smart new coat of battleship grey primer – now we've got to turn her over.*

smooth hull has one redeeming feature. It does not require much brainpower. I found the only approach was to rig myself up with gloves, mask, earmuffs, etc., switch on the grinder and think of – well never mind what I thought of, you choose your own distractions. Even this job can be rendered less hateful by rigging a counterpoise system to relieve the heavy weight of the angle grinder. The grinder with this system is almost weightless and I found that I could grind away for hours instead of just a few minutes.

SHOT BLASTING THE HULL PRIOR TO PAINTING

Shot blasting the hull was the next step in our programme. This is essential to clear off mill scale and provide a key for paint. As the hull had been built upside down our reasoning was that the abrasive used inside the boat would fall out and not require shovelling out afterwards. However as experience proved that abrasive may be recycled several times it could be economic to blast with the hull upright. Shot blasting is an expensive business costing £9 – 15 per hour plus grit or sand, which is around £2 per hundredweight bag. Without recycling any abrasive a 40-foot boat will use well over 50 bags. It obviously pays to rig tarpaulins etc. to catch the abrasive for re-use. Having tried copper slag, grit and sand, we found that sand gave the best profile for painting being like fine emery paper.

Shot blasting is not technically difficult and having spent over £500 in fees I would advocate doing the job yourself by hiring a machine. Provided you remember that a blast of sand is as dangerous as a machine gun. Shirehire as mentioned before, have just acquired one for which the rate is £45 per week.

Make sure that the machine and the compressor are man enough for a big job. With a $^3/_8$ in nozzle and a hefty compressor you should blast clean about 50 sq ft per hour to a good standard. All tools etc should be cleared away before this operation as the billowing clouds of dust penetrate everywhere. An industrial vacuum cleaner to clean out the boat afterwards is a good idea.

The hull was then primed immediately with zinc grey primer. This was expensive also and cost us over £200. The only alternative seems to be to leave the outside of the hull to be shot blasted after completion of all internal welding then blast and apply epoxy paint direct to the blasted surface.

The technology of paint systems like many other aspects of boat building, is a subject by itself and demands hours of study. I have found the people in the technical department of International Paints Ltd. and Berger Paints Ltd., very helpful and kind in their advice.

Rob and I felt proud of our upside down little ship in her smart new coat of battleship grey. The next problem was suddenly upon us.

How could we turn her over?

Chapter 4

Rolling Over to Finish off

Turning over a steel hull weighing 6 tons in the confined space of a barn, was a problem that Joshua Slocum did not have to face. But I'm sure he would have made light of the task which occupied the thoughts of Rob and I for countless hours....

Two crane drivers having inspected the job had withdrawn due to lack of sufficient headroom to work their jibs. It was up to us. As there was too little room to roll the boat over we had to devise a way of suspending her whilst we dismantled and removed the building jig, itself weighing one and a half tons. The hull must then be rotated in only one and a half times her own width without risk of bringing down the barn roof, or damaging the vessel. Which of the two had priority in my mind I'm not prepared to say.

To my surprise, the job, which had caused me, more concern than any other went smoothly and entirely without mishap. It was accomplished with the help of methods used by the ancients for moving large objects and for which I have a growing respect.

The vessel was supported at either end by a massive wooden beam whilst the jig was dismantled and removed from beneath her. The beams were then lowered on jacks to rest on wooden rollers, pine logs about 8in in diameter, which themselves rested on boards so that they would roll more easily.

The hull was winched on these rollers to one side of the barn, where a derrick had been constructed by lashing together two telegraph poles from which hung a block and tackle of 2 ½ tons capacity. The derrick was securely guyed at each side and to the rear. Old tyres and a straw bale were packed under the edge of the hull furthest from the derrick in order to spread the load as the hull was rolled onto its side. All the angle-bar cross braces had been left in the boat to provide athwartships stiffening during the roll. The lifting hook was shacked to a multiple rope strop passing around several cross-braces and the lift began, the greatest weight being taken at first by the poles in compression. It was pointed out at an early stage, that Chris, the man operating the lifting tackle had to stand directly beneath the upraised edge of the hull which swayed ponderously as the timber poles creaked ominously. It was apparent that if anything were to suddenly let go then severe damage would be done to Chris and possibly to the edge of the boat if it were to strike a sharp bone!

Accordingly a safety harness was rapidly acquired. It was of the type used for hauling unconscious men from deep sewers after being overcome by gas. Wearing this apparatus the redoubtable Chris was hoisted up on high where he

Rolling her over; the cross-braces were left in for stiffening. She filled the barn to the brim and poor old Chris had to dangle from the roof.

dangled from one of the roof trusses in the barn smoking a woodbine and hauling on the lifting chain without a care in the world. A large audience had gathered to watch the spectacle. Advice and fag ends flew thick and fast. However the chains clanked merrily and the side of the vessel rose higher and higher until resting on her side she looked immense.

There being too little room to roll the hull right over the next step was to winch the side of the hull resting on the padded floor towards the foot of the derrick. To avoid the vessel suddenly moving in any direction if anything slipped several restraining ropes led to secure anchorage at various points.

As the lower edge of the hull was drawn sideways the top edge was lowered away gently until at last there she stood looking even at this stage as the late R. D. Culler said of his *Spray*, *"plain majestic"*.

That night I had rather more than my fair share of Newcastle Brown ale. The next day I felt somewhat unwell but I am told that I went down to the barn at least a dozen times – I do wish that people would not exaggerate – to gaze at our creation which had taken precisely one year to accomplish. Turn over date being New Years Day 1981.

Laurels were something on which we were not anxious to rest. However fate took a hand at this stage and the delay occurred while I went into hospital for an operation. On my bedside locker was a tottering pile of boating books, P.B.O.'s etc which helped to while away the time and ease my frustration.

The next best thing to boatbuilding is reading about it!

Ballast and bulkheads were the next items on the agenda. During my incapacity Rob had been cutting out some of the bulkheads from 3mm plate. Complicated shapes these, requiring much thought, but easy enough to install on a steel boat by welding to the frames.

However it was sensible to install the ballast in the steel box keel whilst the ship was relatively empty. When I discovered that the cost of proprietary ballast was over £100

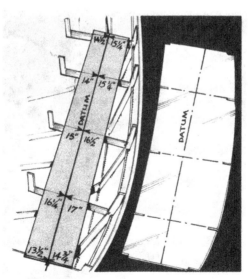

Cutting off the side deck beams and the method we used for laying out the plate templates

500lbs of ballast on the way up! Half a dustbin full of steel shot in cement at around 320lb. per cu. ft. and The chain locker bulkhead welded to the frames. Note the longitudinal rods at the chines.

per ton, I did not require a degree in maths to realise that my 7 ½ tons would cost me some £500 more than I could lay my hands on by legal means.

I had fallen into the habit of putting out enquiries through acquaintances, no matter how casually met. Reactions can be unpredictable when one sidles up to a chap at the bar and whispers, with a conspiratorial glance over the shoulder, worthy of Long John Silver seeking Blind Pew. "*Do ee know where I can lay me hands on a bit o' decent ballast?*" One can easily be carried away by this boatbuilding lark and permanently damage one's reputation for mental stability. Nevertheless, occasionally you will bring off a coup.

A splendid fellow, chance met, just happened to know where there was 7 tons of used steel shot from a shot blasting plant at a local factory awaiting disposal on the tip. Too dirty for recycling but perfect for mixing with cement and pouring into the keel of a steel boat! Mine for the carting away. Apparently this stuff is widely available at large engineering works. Make your enquiries well in advance so that arrangements can be made for the material to be stored or collected over a period.

The actual job of mixing the 7 tons of ballast, lifting it into the boat and installing it in the keel was one that I viewed with foreboding. But it was accomplished easily in one week with the help of my stalwart sons well primed with dandelion and burdock. The pinhead sized steel shot was mixed at around 4 to 1 with cement into a sloppy mix using a small hired mixer.

A rope corset was made for a galvanized steel dustbin which, when filled half full with each mix, weighed nearly 500lbs. This was hoisted by chain block and tackle into the boat, positioned over the particular keel section to be filled by sideways pull using two-part tackle, and then poured into place. The density of the compound is about 320lbs per cu ft. Some 20% of the ballast was reserved for trimming after fitting out and launching.

The deck beams, which on our boat are 2 ½ x ¼ steel section had been rolled to the correct radius by a local engineering shop, after attempts to perform this function with a sledge hammer and left my hands tingling for days. The deck beams were welded into place without a problem. A batten was used to ensure a fair curve in those beams which were cut short to meet the side of the coach roof. Use of the batten gave a curve varying slightly from measurements taken from the plan.

The cut out centres of the deck beams were to make the coach roof beams which were welded onto uprights forming the shape of the cabin sides, again making frequent use of the fairing batten to ensure even curves.

Measure twice and cut once is a useful adage to remember when cutting out complicated shapes such as the steel bulkheads. The installation of bulkheads is relatively straightforward if several pairs of hands are available, or if the sheet is slung from a gantry, or better still both. The spirit level and rule must be in constant use to ensure correct positioning before the welder renders the installation permanent.

Our bulkheads were stiffened with angle-bar from the cross-braces of the now redundant building jig. Waste not want not, says I.

The fitting of the side-decks required cutting out intricate shapes to exact measurements, as each sheet had to be slotted to receive two 2 ½ x ³⁄₈ in frames on one side and the cabin side uprights on the other. This was done by laying a strip of hardboard roughly down the centre of the position the side deck would occupy; drawing in the position of the beams on the hardboard and also a datum line from which exact measurements were taken along each beam and marked on the strip. The measurements were transferred to steel sheet and all the dots were joined up using a fairing batten. This technique worked well for us.

It was a great luxury when the side decks were installed. Walking around the vessel became a pleasure rather than an obstacle course. Even Jason, our spaniel, came up the ladder for a stroll round the deck with characteristic swagger. His enthusiasm for climbing ladders became a passion, until he fell of the top rung one day and dealt a severe blow to a piece of scrap metal with the side of his head. I notice lately though, that he is becoming venturesome again. Some dogs never learn!

In order to bring the job forward at this stage, Rob enlisted the temporary help of two accomplices rejoicing in the names of Barney and Twig. Now although this sounds like a music hall double act, Twig is an expert welder and Barney is an expert at painting spiders, grinding dust, tools and welding gloves. Nothing is immune from Barney's brush. All have been given a lavish coat of Galvafroid.

Barney's job was to grind off and prime the newly welded seams on the decks and coach roofs. The trio worked as a team, Rob cutting out the steel plates using hardboard templates where required, Twig welding them into position whilst Barney followed, grinding off and priming. We chose to use the standard Galvafroid for this purpose. The epoxy based Galvafroid E.V. would probably have been better but as only small quantities were being used at irregular intervals the waste would have been considerable as the pot life of the two part mix is relatively brief.

In a few weeks this threesome completed the decking, the coach roofs, the cockpit and the enormous amount of fillet welding round the deck edges where the MIG welder really came into its own. Steel tube 3in diameter has been cut into four lengthways to form the round edge of the cockpit which are to be preferred to sharp edges for comfort, safety and aesthetic reasons.

We now have a complete hull with all bulkheads fitted and although I says it as shouldn't, for a bunch of amateurs she doesn't look at all bad!

Chapter 5

Foam Lining for a Snug Interior

No one could accuse Joshua Slocum of molly-coddling himself. Built in the days of wooden ships and iron men; accommodation in the old *Spray* was Spartan in the extreme. Slocum dismisses the subject of fitting out in less than eleven lines of his book, which gives some indication of its place on his scale of priorities.

Fortunately Bruce Roberts, in his version of the *Spray* caters for creature comforts somewhat more indulgently, and Rob and I set about filling that great cavern of a hull to make her as snug and cosy as two amateurs could devise.

Old Slocum's wraith hung around us as we worked, so it seemed, and if he raised his craggy eyebrows in disbelief at our provision for a shower rather than an enamel bowl, and a freezer in substitute for his cask of salt beef, he nodded his grim approval as the framing for the galley, bunks and lockers etc, was fashioned from steel angle bar welded into the structure of the boat, giving additional strength to an already rugged vessel.

An exciting an absorbing stage this, as steel is a material which allows considerable latitude for indulging one's fancy in variations on the basic layout so long as due regard is paid to strength. Rapid and satisfying progress is possible in cutting and welding in the furniture framework. However much time spent scratching one's head and pondering over unforeseen problems. What height and angle does the back of a seat require to provide acceptable comfort? How far can the average person reach into a locker? What height worktops?

My steel tape rule was a constant companion and curious glances embarrassed me often when I was caught out surreptitiously measuring seats in pubs. Hieroglyphics on beer mats all very well but I found a much better source of reference while looking through a pile of old P.B.O.'s. Mike Saunders' article *Cabins Made To Measure* in the November 1979 issue also Ian Nicholson's *Boat Data* book is an absolute mine of information.

It is a difficult feat, if amusing to the unexpected observer, to attempt to measure whilst lying (like Albert's lion) in various recumbent positions, how far upwards and outwards one's buttocks protrude. This in order to ensure that allowing a generous margin for error (or more generous buttocks) one is not snagged by the overhanging backrest support during one's slumbers or other nocturnal activities.

It is accepted that single berths are more comfortable at sea but a double may be useful in port. Accordingly a cunning arrangement was devised whereby the backrests dividing two settees and the pilot berth outboard of them were made so that they could be removed, converting two single berths into two cosy doubles.

The interior structure starts to take shape – here the framework for the galley and nav' area is under construction. The angle will be finished off with timber.

The chemicals used to form the foam are dangerous and proper equipment and safeguards must be employed. Leave it to the experts...

In the meantime I had been in search of a rare-subspecies of diesel mechanic. He must be of sound judgement that he should not leave unsuspected faults lurking in my engine, nor yet so hypercritical that he would throw away slightly worn parts with many thousands of hours work left in them, and cost me more of my dwindling resources than necessary.

MARINISING A DIESEL

After a long search I found Roy, who in two weekends and with baffling dexterity, stripped down and rebuilt my Ford ex-tractor engine is now engaged in its marinisation with parts from Lancing Marine of Portslade. As I am uncommonly obtuse in the way of mechanics, Mike Bellamy stayed very late at his office when I collected the parts, attempting to explain how they all went together.

The cutting out of the opening for the forward hatch, the companion way hatch and the ports and scuppers was accomplished without problem using the acetylene torch. In cutting out the scuppers I erred on the generous side. *If Mr Green invites himself aboard*, said an old sailor, *you don't want him hanging around trying to find the way off.* Sounds like good advice!

The appearance of the port lights can make or mar a vessel so I cut out templates of hardboard and taped them in place on the cabin sides adjusting the position, shape and size until they looked right.

We wanted plenty of light down below but ready-made port lights of the size we required were beyond my means so we elected to make our own.

After a great deal of thought and experiment we eventually evolved a pattern, which looked superb and cost very little.

The glazing material is Makrolon 'a space age' polycarbonate plastic. It is virtually unbreakable and yet can be drilled and cut using ordinary tools without splitting. It will conform to a curve but is not so resistant to abrasion as glass, so may need replacing after a few years. In a fixed coach-roof deadlight the glazing is most easily removed from outside.

The problems with external glazing are:

a) How to bridge the gap twixt hull and panelling inside, and
b) How to avoid the crude appearance of some vessels which merely have the glazing bolted to the outside of the hull.

The first problem was solved by developing an idea in Mike Pratt's book *Own A Steel Boat* but using pieces of solid elm 1 ½ in thick instead of plywood. The aperture for the port was cut out with a jigsaw then the inside given an attractive profile with a router. My initial intention was to finish off the outside of the ports with a mahogany surround rebated to the thickness of the glazing. However my eye lighted by chance one day upon a small section of the Yellow Pages headed *Brass Founders and Finishers*. Expecting all sorts of problems and like the King's wife, more in hope than expectation, I made a telephone call and was invited to visit Severn Castings Ltd., where I was greeted by Mr Bill and his two sons, Mike and John.

Not only was my small order welcomed, to my surprise an immediate grasp was obtained of my requirements. So rare these days and one advantage of the small firm where you talk to the organ grinder...

In most places all that is required is an original item or a pattern of wood or plaster. Castings can be done in brass, bronze or aluminium – marine grade L10 if required. Bear in mind that there is a shrinkage of 1.5% which in many cases does not matter.

At this moment a ship's bell with her name on it is being cast for our little ship. Possibilities are endless. Within days of making my plywood pattern I was summoned to watch the first pour. Entering the foundry was to step back a century or more. Sulphurous fumes stung the nostrils. The roaring blast of the furnace and the searing flames from the molten metal within the pot announced that all was ready. A long handled scoop was dipped into the fiery fluid and its contents poured carefully into the mould of fine damp sand from which clouds of steam erupted. Later the same day and less than ten days after my first enquiry, I received twelve beautifully burnished port surrounds at a cost of just over a fiver each. How's that for service. Severn Castings Ltd. Tel. Telford 613873. The 'Yellow Pages' of your local directory or see under Castings non ferrous in Sells Marine Market from Sells House, 39 East Street, Epsom, Surrey. This book is worth its weight in 22ct to the boat builder – being a directory of thousands of manufacturers and other bodies useful to the boating fraternity.

'Steel boats die from the inside outwards'. Thus spake the voices of authority. Due apparently to condensation

forming in hidden crevices behind panels etc. On the strong recommendation of Ian Nicholson and Mike Pratt in their books we elected to have the inside of *Ospray* sprayed with polyurethane foam, which is the most efficient of all commercially available insulation materials having a 'K' value of 0.023W/m deg C. This material is a two-part blend of chemicals which, when combined with a blowing agent, forms a structure of closed-cell plastic spheres which sticks with remarkable tenacity to solid surfaces, forms an impermeable barrier to water, and greatly reduces heat loss. One inch thickness is ample for insulating a boat. Another great advantage is sound insulation, especially on steel vessels where, if someone drops a spanner on deck, one emerges from within with a dazed expression like Quasimodo from his belfry *"It's the bells you know"*.

This is a job for the professional requiring expensive equipment. Tony and Steve from CAS Urethanes Ltd., who supplied the lowest quote, did a splendid job or our forty footer in one day, including masking off the furniture framing which had already been installed. It may pay to do this in advance, but be thorough. I didn't bother having the bulkheads masked off and had several hours work scraping off flecks of foam.

The effect, on completion of the job, was dramatic. The foam has a most attractive surface like drifted snow but is a warm biscuit colour, which transforms a cold steel hull into a cosy den. It is almost a shame to cover the inside with panelling. You didn't have it all your own way Josh Slocum! The cost of insulating a boat with one-inch thick foam varies between £6 and £11 per square metre of surface.

I was well pleased with the job done by CAS Urethanes Ltd., whose address is Mill House, Hensall, Nr Goole and ask for Mike Heron. Other firms worth trying are Gulf Insulation Ltd., Cheltenham or Rubroid Insulation Services, Trafford Park, Manchester. Or try the Yellow Pages for someone nearer.

My earliest attempts at carpentry met with resounding failure. My opinion of myself as a tolerable jungle carpenter,

Insulating a quarter berth with sprayed-on foam. The surface is rather like textured 'snow'. Some idea of the thickness can be gained from the window cut-outs.

I found, had been somewhat optimistic. Measure twice and cut once is a useful adage which I have mentioned before – and will probably mention again – I measured twice and still found it necessary to cut about fourteen times! Mind you I am improving. Of that there is no doubt. There is only one way you can go when you start from the bottom. I now turn out work which I not only permit people to see but I hope they will do so. I fitted a mini bulkhead partition in the galley the other day which I cut out of solid elm 1½ inch thick. Now this piece has such voluptuous curves which follow the grain so sweetly that I sat back amazed at my handiwork and barely made it to the pub before time was shouted. I wouldn't have cared anyway.

Rob has made a fine set of companionway steps from beautifully figured elm. These are strong enough to use for storming the Bastille and beneath each step is a little locker for binoculars, flares etc.

Confidentially, carpentry is becoming my new obsession. Boat building is like that. Not one obsession but many. I go into a pub and absolutely crave for someone to strike up a conversation about carpentry. But they never do.

And it all started like this. A friend of mine mentioned that an old lady of her ken was anxious to find a good home for 'some tools' belonging to her late husband, whom she referred to affectionately as Old Clay. I went to see Mrs Clay and a bargain was soon struck – in fact we became fast friends.

Now it turns out that H G Clay, (which was stamped on all his tools) had been a carpenter in the RAF where near enough was not good enough. This was evident by this remarkable man's tools. And what a set of tools! Never in my wildest dreams did I dream of owning such treasures. This man loved his trade with a passion and I spend many hours marvelling and pondering over the purpose of each item. All lovingly maintained. The wooden handles of chisels, mallets and saws were slick with linseed oil. The spoke shaves were each wrapped in soft cloth. The chisels were not only capable of cutting wood but were eager and desirous of doing so. The planes and there were many of them, would with the merest pressure curl over such beautiful wafers of wood that one could write poetry about them. Save money where you can but buy the best tools you can afford. Poor tools produce poor work, take my word for it. Put out feelers well in advance. You may be lucky as I was and find a treasure chest. The incredible thing is that the handling of these tools has inspired me a veritable duffer in this field, to strive for the perfection that was demanded by 'Old Clay'. Often have I been tempted to say to myself, that'll do. Only to imagine the old mans tut tut over my shoulder. I still can't match H G Clay's standards but I have the feeling that he may award a few points for trying.

Teak and mahogany are the conventional timbers for high-class finish of yacht furniture because of their beauty and durability. However these timbers are becoming very expensive. With modern treatments and finishes many alternatives are possible. There are a considerable variety of lesser known, cheaper but often exquisite timbers available to amateurs which will add charm and character to the home built boat. I will tell you about them sometime.

Chapter 6

Jumbling at Beaulieu

Aladdin's Cave. A treasure trove. The happy hunting ground for boaty bargains. The metaphors fly thick and fast in an effort to describe a day at Beaulieu boat jumble. The grandest day I've had out in years. This annual event is on Lord Montague's estate in Hampshire, snuggling amongst the ancient oaks of a hunting forest that was 'new' a long time ago, in a corner of England locked fast in matters maritime where the mists of time swirl and the past lives comfortably with the present. Where gnarled oaks bearing the century's old scars of amputations shelter saplings who need never fear the woodman's axe recruiting grown frames.

Boats jostling on the tide like farmers at a fair, oak rubbing a friendly strake with polyester. Cosy old taverns whose low beams have brushed the tricorn hat and whose floors have known the ring of the wooden leg, serving, without a blush scampi in the basket. This is the setting for a weekend orgy in nauticalia. Splendid though the setting, the jewel in the centre is undoubtedly the Beaulieu Boat Jumble.

Un-missable in my estimation by any paid up member of the boating fraternity. Browsers, builders, buyers or boat dwellers. Something here for everyone. Row upon row of open air stalls and marquees, acres of them right for barter and bargaining, from rusty relics to triple plated chrome. The variety and volume of boaty gear is breathtaking. I exaggerate not.

During the day I acquired by a great deal of hard and jocular haggling a lorry load of loot which included a 65lb CQR anchor for £21, a 45lb Danforth anchor, slightly bent for £17. A tenner bought a 25lb Fishermans anchor of poetic proportions. A huge pair of Gibb winches built like

Swiss watches but powerful enough to shift the Rock of Gibraltar came eventually for £90. The modern equivalent would have cost me almost a grand. Few could pass that stall without trying those bronze beauties and marvelling at their powers.

My lad Jonathon and I had been kindly allowed to share a stall of my good friend Patrick – and another *Spray* builder – there is a lot of it about that means *Spray* building. Accordingly we had travelled south on Saturday in time to take our spaniels Jason and Misty Blue for a midnight scamper in the vastness of the New Forest. The dogs thought this was the Promised Land, being bursting at the seams with rabbits in bramble bushes and other jolly diversions essential for the quality of life.

We settled down for the night in our cosy candlelit van, with a spaniel each for a foot warmer. Five star hotels are all very well but.....

The day dawned bright and clear. The day break drive from the campsite, of which there wee many, was through open heaths and wood a-sparkle with dew and roamed freely by herds of wild ponies and the occasional deer.

Being registered vendors we were on site very early. The place was a hive of activity. A constant miscellany of transport poured into the site for many had arrived the previous day and had already set out their wares. These folk were mostly to be seen clasping a strong brew in one hand and poking with early morning vacuity at bacon sizzling over a roaring primus. Soon they were knocking out bacon butties with the practised deftness of a brickie, hoping to tice out occupants of vans, still slumbering among intriguing heaps of chandlery. Camaraderie and the smell of bacon were in the air. I confess to being a-tingle with anticipation.

Many of the stallholders evidently knew each other well enough to hurl jibes and insults across the valley. Wares, boats and personal habits came under broadside and counter broadside. It seemed to me there had been some carousal the night before.

Now Patrick is a self confessed sluggard in the morning and I was well into my second cup of rosie lee before he roared in with his entourage which put me in mind of Bertram Mills on the move. However the stall was set up in record time and Jonathan was left in charge of our wee corner whilst I went in search of bargains. To use the idiom of our trans-Atlantic cousins I felt like a kid at a candy stall.

In a trice I was back, tottering under several miles of warp and a 65lb CQR, which swung about and threatened to remove my teeth at every step. Who ever designed CQR anchors aught to be made to carry one in eternal perdition.

Dumping my wares back at base camp and barking orders not to sell them unless at a good profit – I was soon off again like a lamplighter, to pick up the threads on a bit of haggling with a stall holder on Row M for a splendid hefty pair of davits which would look just right on a rugged *Ospray*. The asking price was £45. My opening offer was

Seemingly stout enough to lift the *Mary Rose, these handsome davits proved to be just right for the back end of Ospray.*

£25 was treated with the scorn I expected. My new improved offer of £28 did not do much better but I thought I detected a glimmer of interest. "*Oh my eyes and my liver*" cried this Dickensian rolling his eyes heavenwards. "*Cost you a fortune to have made*".

An hour and an enamel kettle later I staggered back to base camp on the verge of collapse under a pair of davits which would have raised the *Mary Rose*, after parting with £31 to our friend on Row M, who asked if I would kindly visit him in the workhouse on Christmas Day.

This protracted bargaining is absolutely hell on the nerves; you feel sure you will arrive back on the scene to find some affluent swine shelling out for some treasure which you have just convinced yourself is the chance of a lifetime.

Meanwhile, back at the ranch, my son Jon had been doing well and was gleefully stuffing his already bulging pockets with notes from the sale of *our* accumulated boating debris. For instance I had sometime before attended a liquidation sale of a firm who had gone to the wall and in a rash moment had bought for £80 a bulk load of 98 used life jackets, thereby earning for myself the reputation of the worlds greatest pessimist. These were now selling faster than hot cakes at £4 each. A steering pedestal, which I had decided, was not hefty enough to swing *Ospray's* huge bulk pulled in the £65 that I had been delighted to pay for it months before.

This new found wealth lent wings to my heels and pausing only to treat Jonathan to a brace of hamburgers being momentarily overcome by generosity, I was away again to feast my eyes on prized sextants which had known 10,000 sunrises. Ships bells whose tongues had waken cold sailors to the dread of the horn. Anchors, strong armed and steadfast as the sailors hoped on many a lee shore. I saw a ship's wheel among many, a thing of exquisite beauty of form and colour, the patina on wood and bronze having a dark glow that could come only from long use and loving care. I jibbed at the price of £120 but having since had many regrets.

My next buy was a bag full of Tufnol blocks from one well known firm which had just merged with another and was selling old stock at under half price.

This was one of many trade stands offering goods at greatly reduced prices, seconds, shop-soiled, and end of range items and bargains galore for a practical boat owner.

The whole affair was a well-run, jolly day out with refreshments, stalls, and toilet facilities and so forth. A day to make firm friends. A day for sweaters and Jeans. The highlight of my day came as the light was drawing to a close when I struck a last minute bargain with a Cornish man whose accent was straight out of *Treasure Island*. I spied a bunch of lignum vitae deadeyes being loaded into his van. The purpose of these objects agleam with linseed oil was to me somewhat obscure but our Cornish friend soon had me convinced of the impropriety of rigging a copy of the old *Spray* with anything so vulgar as rigging screws. *"A little bit like going to the Lord Mayor's banquet wearing Jeans"* he said.

One thing you must not fail to do before embarking on an expedition to Beaulieu and the Solent area. Make a list of everything you need and make detailed notes of all measurements or you will end up, as I was, wracked with frustration. There was this beautifully made Appledore reefing gear, a great chunk of gleaming bronze going for a knock down price. And there was I not knowing the size of my boom! Needless to say, someone else knew the size of his, and snapped it up.

Mind you another great chunk of gleaming bronze did become mine a fortnight later. This was a 24-inch adjustable pitch propeller and its ancillary control gear on the stall of Yot-Grot. Now my knowledge of these intriguing devices was bordering on the abysmal so what did I do? I scurried 200 miles back home and waded through about 8 years' PBOs to find that:

a) A prop, which can be feathered fore and aft, can increase sailing speed by one knot.

b) Does not require a gearbox.
c) Can be adjusted to give maximum punch at low engine speeds when motor sailing avoiding the need to throttle up to 'catch up with the sails'.

A telephone bargain being struck resulted in another 400 mile round trip to collect my prize. However whilst in the area, a Mecca of the boat builder, I winkled out a few more little hot spots for bargains. From Yot-Grot, Lymington, a heavy bronze halliard winch from the legendary Merriman and Co., for £9. Jerry Foulks' Emporium on the wharf at Bursledon provided two bronze sheet winches - bright green and seized up solid - cost at £10 each plus a couple hours' work to strip down and rebuild. At Harry Smith's Belsize boat breakers a mountain of gear await your probing little fingers. I bore away a mighty two-handled windlass, with a musical clank to the pawls, which would have delighted old Josh Slocum with his formidable 175lb. anchor. Quite a handful I imagine even in the days of wooden ships and iron men. He reckoned, he slept easy with such ground tackle down and I hope he still does.

This time I may be a bit better organised, combining these expeditions into one glorious long weekend spree. And above all I must measure up first.

Chapter 7

First Find your Tree

Timber! The very name has a ring to it. What is it and where does it come from? How many of us have wiped tears of mirth and pathos from our eyes when some city child states, with wide-eyed conviction, that milk comes from the milkman, yet have looked no further than the timber yard for our wood? Let us not be so swift to snigger.

But surely boatbuilding timber comes from remote equatorial jungles or vast sub-arctic forests? Or at the very least from hallowed stands of centuries-old oak, doesn't it? Well *'It ain't necessarily so'*. That is an illusion fostered by the demands of commerce, which require large quantities, and regular supplies of gradeable timber. The main supply of hull timbers will continue to come from those traditional sources with all the professional backup skills of selection and grading.

But with modern preservatives and protective coatings there is room for a radical re-think by the amateur and small-time boat builder, and there is tremendous scope for increased use of homegrown timbers, especially in fitting out. Some are well known. There are others whose uses have been almost forgotten, but which were once highly prized for their special qualities and beauty.

"My axe felled a stout oak tree nearby for a keel," writes Slocum as though he had just slipped down to the ironmongers for a pound of nails. Later *"The much esteemed stem piece was from the butt of the smartest kind of pasture oak. Better timber for a ship than pasture white oak never grew"*.

Now I suppose it would be expecting too much of providence to find you had the very smartest oak at the bottom of the garden menacing your neighbour's greenhouse, but the young George Washington was not the last to chop down a cherry tree. It may surprise you to know that cherry was treasured by cabinetmakers of old for its breathtaking lustre. You may find it easier to fib about it than George. Perhaps you could say it was diseased or under mining the drains.

The common old damson tree can yield timber, which is nothing short of exotic, being dense, and lustrous with burgundy coloured streaks running through. A few selected lockers or drawers faced with wood of distinction and character rarely found on production boats.

Acquiring a stock of timber is, like many other things, more difficult in its conception than execution. However it does entail a little more bother then picking up the phone and placing an order.

A productive source is to be found by scanning the advert columns of your local paper under *produce or logs for sale*. Now log merchants work in several ways. The two main ones being:

a) To work independently clearing individual tress for small stands of timber and scrub which is of no commercial interest, or

b) To work in conjunction with large scale felling operations whereby an arrangement is made to take the lop and top from the main contractors.

Either way you may be onto a winner because what you are interested in is the log merchant's problem. Logs that are too small for commercial timber but too big to be used for firewood without splitting. Splitting logs is mighty hard work. Splitting elm logs is murder. Quite probably this occupation would be the ultimate deterrent in remote penal colonies were it not for the Geneva Conventions regarding crimes against humanity!

For a price ranging upwards from £20 per ton you ought to arrive at an amicable arrangement with your local friendly log merchant who may well be persuaded by the price of a few pints to deliver your logs direct to you local friendly sawmill for conversion.

My particular LF sawmill is a firm named ETC of Ellesmere, Shropshire where the very real Doug McCoy is uncommonly helpful and converts my timber without fuss into any thickness for just under £2 per cu ft. This firm can also supply English hardwoods at extremely competitive prices either rough sawn or dressed to your requirements. For a paltry fee this can also be treated against decay and insect attack for use anywhere on the boat including, I am told, under water.

The last few years have seen the re-emergence of timber as an engineering material, partly due to the development of materials giving effective and almost infinite protection from rot and or moisture absorption. This may be by impregnation with chemicals which have a residual effect against the organisms causing decay, the modern alternative to creosote being somewhat more subtle, less pungent and more compatible with decorative finishes.

The alternative method is the physical exclusion of moisture. The most effective way of achieving this end is by *totally* encapsulating each piece of timber in resin as in the WEST System as advertised in this journal. Horses for courses obviously. The degree of protection depends on access to every surface of the timber, and hence on the situation of its intended use.

The longer and thicker the logs you send to the sawmill the more flexible the use of the yielded timber, but any log over three feet long and six inches thick may be considered. When the boards are collected from the mill they must be put 'in stick' for seasoning. For this you require spacer sticks sawn to even thicknesses of about 1inch. The boards are stacked in layers as they come from the log so that grain may be matched if required. Spacer sticks should be about 2 feet apart. The stack should be covered to exclude rain but not air, which should circulate freely. The time for air-drying varies from 4 to 18 months for timber not more than 1 ½in thick. This should preferably be followed by a short period in a warmer (drier) atmosphere just prior to use.

If like me, you have some primeval hankering to follow in old Slocum's footsteps and fell your own timber then why not? The price you may pay of being regarded as a crank is small against the wealth of earthy satisfaction gained from such a fundamental action as cutting down a tree to build a boat.

This is an entirely reasonable proposition providing you approach the subject with due humility. You MUST start small. DO NOT attempt as your first job to fell a forest giant overhanging an 1100-watt cable feeding the Soviet Embassy. Well you can if you like, but please refrain from mentioning my name in the subsequent trial. Even experienced timber men are heavily ensured against tricky jobs.

You can't beat a nice piece of home grown elm. Use it for good-looking and durable work-surfaces, although wide planks can warp unless well braced. To saw it up, I use the coach roof as a carpenter's workbench....

A chain saw is a DANGEROUS implement. Learn how to use one and treat it always with respect. WEAR PROTECTIVE CLOTHING. Heavy boots, gloves, safety helmet with visor or goggles. HAVE THE PROPPER GEAR FOR THE JOB. If directional control of fall is required you may need ropes, wedges and a winch, which must, of course, be made fast to a secure anchor point such as another tree. Trees presenting serious complications and all very large trees should be left to the professional. The toppling of a big tree is an awesome sight. However the first ominous creak from a swaying leviathan which appears, because of a playful gust of wind to be giving serious consideration to demolishing the vicarage, will keep you in nightmares for years. TAKE NO CHANCES AND TACKLE THE JOB THUS.

1. Check the weight and lean of the tree. Always try to fell a tree as close as possible to its natural line.

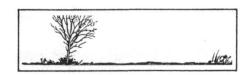

2. Clear away obstructions from the line of fall.

3. *Clear debris from base of tree and any limbs below head height.*

4. *Clear obstacles from escape route, which should be clear of any possible line of drop.*

5. *Start the chain saw by placing the engine on firm ground and placing the right foot in the handle. Holding the front grip with the left hand whilst pulling the started cord with the right.*

6. *Make the top cut of the wedge first at a downward angle of about 45 degrees extending about ¼ of the diameter of the trunk. The bottom cut should be straight in to meet with the top cut. The wedge shaped opening should exactly face the direction of fall.*

7. *The final cut should be an inch or two above the bottom line of the wedge. Cut in towards the wedge keeping the hinge thickness even along its length. As soon as the tree starts to move withdraw the saw, stop the engine and step backwards and to one side in case of kick back. DO NOT run away unless in danger.*

WHICH WOOD?

Here is a summary of the character and quality of some of the hardwoods you may come across.

PEAR: Pale pinkish brown with a very fine texture. Capable of taking a fine finish. Needs slow and careful seasoning. Turns extremely well and was used for drawing instruments and cabinetwork.

ELM: Prominent grain with beautiful figuring. Extremely hard to split hence its use for the seats of Windsor chairs widely used for solid furniture and coffins!

CHERY: Dense hardwood capable of taking high finish once eagerly sought for small items of high-class furniture. Attractive figure often with flecks of green or gold, which has been likened to forest sunlight.

LABURNUM: Often cut down in gardens because the black seeds are mildly poisonous to children. It's an ill wind that blows no good. Stable in damp conditions and is extremely attractive, being chocolate brown with cream flecks and stripes. Widely used for decorative purposes, small drawer fronts etc. and for the chanters of bagpipes. *Tak note ye Scotsmen.*

WALLNUT: "*A woman, a spaniel and a walnut tree, the more you beat 'em, the better they be*", says an old proverb by some medieval chauvinist. Not withstanding centuries of apparent abuse, the walnut continues to yield one of the world's outstanding timbers used for fine furniture and quality gunstocks.

YEW: Although botanically a soft wood, you will discover just how soft it is if you try to cut it with a blunt saw. Yew is a hard lustrous wood, red-brown heartwood with pale cream sap wood of great beauty in appearance and stable in use having great strength and elasticity hence its use for longbows, the weapon that is.

SYCAMORE: Pale creamy-brown timber taking a fine finish and especially suitable in the galley areas, in view of its bright clean appearance. Also ideal for deck head and wall (ceiling) panelling where a light and airy effect is required.

LOCUST: (or False Acacia) A naturally durable hardwood is a beautiful golden-brown with an attractive figure, the wood is extremely resistant to shock and is often used for ship's blocks and wheel spokes but also for high quality furniture.

For further reading I suggest the Observer's Book of Trees and if you really get bitten by the bug, the International Book of Wood will provide countless hours of fascinating browsing. Looking to the future, try to replace or encourage the replacement of any tree removed. Future generations of tree lovers and boat builders will be grateful to you. And why not plant a tree or two to celebrate the birth of a baby? By the time the baby is building boats, the tree will yield a useful volume of timber. What a topic for conversation!

Chapter 8

To Harness the Wind

Joshua Slocum was never a man to waste words. On the subject of rigging his beloved *Spray* he was distinctly parsimonious.

"The mast, a smart New Hampshire spruce, was fitted and likewise all the small appurtenances for a short cruise. Sails were bent and away she flew…"

I suppose the 'small appurtenances' were such trivialities as a boom and a gaff, a few bits and pieces from which to hang the running rigging and the odd shroud to hold up the mast!

One gleans the impression that this was a bit of a job he did to pass the time whilst the kettle boiled. Compare the confident, almost casual approach of this old salt with the feverish intensity of myself, the rank amateur. Up to the eyebrows in reference books, desk bestrewn with slide rules, calculators and sheet upon sheet of paper covered in obscure formulae, the outcome of each being treated with life and death attention to detail.

All I can say, is that having drawn freely on the views of the redoubtable Claude Worth, Dixon Kemp, John Leather and years and years of BPOs, I feel I'm in good company and shall not hesitate to blame them if anything goes wrong. Always assuming I am alive to do so.

Having opted for wooden masts, from a mixture of economic necessity, romanticism and natural inclination, Rob and I (as mentioned in a previous article) had chosen our spars on the hoof from a stand high on a Welsh mountainside.

It is a mighty inspiring spectacle to witness the toppling of a tall tree, arrow straight and selected from thousands for ones main mast, crashing to earth in the resinous hallowed dimness of a mountain forest. That may be accomplished as described in PBO No 197. However, I suggest that it is worth taking pains to ascertain the quality of the timber, as some grown in lowland areas can be spongy and quite unsuitable for spars.

The mast fittings for timber spars are best tailor made, more appropriately blacksmith made and are well within the capacity of a handy chap with a weekend's access to a forge. It is surprising what may be arranged for the price of a few pints. Wink, wink, nudge, nudge....

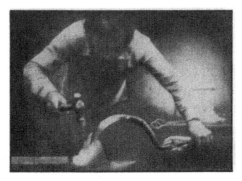

Primeval instincts awakened as the merry clang of the hammer fashions the heat-softened metal into globe-girdling instruments.

The tailor-made mast fittings. Well within the capacity of a handy chap with a weekend's access to a forge.

I must say, as the most ham-fisted blacksmith the good Lord ever let loose with a hammer, that this is *one* satisfying job.

When mild steel is heated to an even cherry red it becomes remarkably obedient. Some primeval instinct is awakened by the searing glare of the forge and the merry clang of the hammer, as blow by blow the heat-softened metal is fashioned into globe girdling instruments to harness the wind. Surely never can there have been a closer conspiracy between the four elements of Aristotle – Earth, Fire, Air and Water.

A forge is deliberately dimly lit. This is so that an accurate assessment can be made of the colour of the metal when heated. This is vital. Too cool and the metal won't be worka- ble, too hot and it will be burned and wasted. A dull cherry red in a dim light is a safe working temperature.

A few simple tips may reduce the failure rate.

1. Mark all sharp bends with a row of centre punch dots – chalk or pencil will disappear in the fire.
2. Hammering will normally stretch hot metal; bear this in mind when measuring up. It is easy to lengthen fittings by ¼ in but very hard to shorten them if too long.
3. Round off all edges, this will help retain the galvanising and reduce chafe on gear.

Vulcan would have given the shirt off his backbone and a share in his deity for a couple of pairs of large size Mole grips. I found that with a pair of these clamped on to each end of a bar I could persuade the metal to curve round a piece of old pipe, the same diameter as the mast, like this:

Before being galvanised the fittings should preferably be shot blasted, both to remove scale and to give a surface like emery, which will hold a thicker coat of protective zinc. Galvanising is surprisingly cheap and for boat fittings costs about 10p per pound. My local firm, Corbetts of Wellington, are uncommonly helpful and will often do work on an, '*in one day and out the next*' basis.

Galvanised fittings painted, after weathering, with a modern paint system are very long lasting and are a fraction of the price of stainless steel. (For more details see Good Old Galvanised by Nigel Warren, in No 154, page 75 – Editor). The masts were seasoned for twelve months during which time they were turned to prevent them taking a set. They were then stripped of bark, which had been left on to slow down the drying rate and minimise splits and shakes.

Traditional methods recommend liberal applications of paraffin and linseed oil mixture during the drying period but I had decided to coat my spars with West epoxy, and oil would have reduced adhesion.

Despite my attempts to control drying rate, several deep longitudinal deep shakes appeared which I filled with epoxy putty before coating the masts with resin, which gave them the amber glow of a newly opened conker!

Various formulae for calculating the diameter of a pole mast suggested that 0.28 in. per foot of height from deck to hounds, tapering to 80% of that at the masthead.

Claude Worth knew a thing or two about wooden spars and well he might for he was in the habit of measuring each spar on every boat he boarded. As a result he concluded that a boom for a yawl or cutter up to 40 feet should be 0.23 in diameter per foot length.

Spar making from seasoned poles is grand work and very satisfying, although electric sander and planer replaced the adze and jackplane of the traditional spar maker. Poles for spars should be chosen so that little except bark and sap wood needs to be removed.

Sitka Spruce has one advantage over Norway in that it has a slower taper and requires less to be shaved from the butt end. The planer should have as long a bed as possible and my method was to set it fairly coarse to begin with. A long straight edge was used constantly to detect lumps and hollows and the spar was rotated a quarter of a turn every few minutes keeping the heart central at each end.

Having thus roughed out the timber, a powerful belt sander was brought into action to round off the spar and remove the many flats left by the planer. It was found to be more effective to use the sander over the curve of the wood rather than lengthways, using a light touch and keeping the machine constantly in motion to avoid making ridges.

On many a velvety June night when the owls call had replaced the cuckoo's shout across the Shropshire meadows, I would pack up my tools and rest awhile on a gleaming white spar. Smothered in shavings, eyes gritty with sawdust, I wouldn't have changed my lot with a king.

My mizzenmast and yard for the lugsail are of Norway spruce from a local wood where my dogs and I have often hunted rabbits. They may well carry a few lead shot as a memento of their former life and perhaps were 'christened' by my territory marking spaniels long before being anointed by the salt spray of the ocean.

Much of my pleasure in boat building stems from this aspect of individuality. Each part of the ship has a tale to tell. Practical, whimsical – occasionally poignant.

How many boats can boast an ecclesiastical bowsprit? *Ospray's* is fashioned from a great beam of pitch pine which once supported a church roof, around which wafted at evening song the hymns and prayers of a congregation who dwelt in an engineless age of sail, when those in peril on the sea beseech the Almighty rather than the RNLI.

The beam which cost me £8 came from a demolition yard crouched amongst the satanic mills of darkest Lancashire.

In the same yard almost buried in the mud, I unearthed a large board for which I was charged a nominal couple of quid by a woodbine-wielding proprietor who was showing signs of anxiety to get off for his Saturday lunchtime pint. This board measured 10 ft 8in x 4 ft 4 in x 1¼ in thick and turned out to be a hooker's bench – what ever that may be - from one of those dark satanic mills and was made from the finest American mahogany! Perfect for *Osprey's* hatches, washboards and many odd bits of trim.

This timber was a source of intrigue and mystery, even romance, for when ever my tools bit into the fibres there arose a miasma distinctly feminine. Some Lancashire lass, may be now a grand mother, in defiance of the swelter and grime of the mill had worn perfume, perhaps as a token of womanhood beneath shawl and clogs as a poke in the eye against the bitter hardness of life, and as she pressed her body in daily toil against her bench the timber absorbed some of the perfume and her indomitable character. I wonder who she was?

The sails of *Osprey* are of Duradon, the synthetic canvas, which looks and smells like the real thing but does not rot. They are the colour of the underside of a mushroom and were bought in response to an advert in PBO from a Harley Street dentist whose boat had lost an argument with an Indonesian reef. Those sails are built like the proverbial brick convenience. In fact we were told, the mainsail is known affectionately as the movver-in-law, following the remark of a London cabbie regarding the vast and lumpy package being lugged across London by a wild looking guy in the wee small hours.

After collecting the sails near Guilford and leaving the warm hospitality of the shipwrecked dentist and his wife, my lad Jon and I plus dogs, set a course even further south to see the tall ships at Southampton. Brake of day among tendrils of sea mist found us unfurling the vast expanse of muvver-in-law on a Southampton car park being quite unable to resist viewing our trophies in daylight.

The spaniels padded and sniffed around expressing profound and joyful interest in every stitch. Passers by on the way to early shift stared and silently accorded us the esteem of belonging to the tall ships pageant, which to my everlasting shame, I made no attempt to deny.

The poor old muvver-in-law has lost a little weight. I sent her back to Lucas the makers, who remember her well. Out of her ample proportions, they made me a 165 sq ft lugsail for the mizzen, such as Slocum chose for the Spray before facing rude Cape Horn and blasting williwaws of Patagonia. However she is still a formidable lady and like all the best mothers-in-law, will require to be treated with respect.

Chapter 9

Ospray Leaves the Nest

In *Ospray's* eyrie all was excitement. The fledgling was about to fly. Doting parents fussed and preened, a lick of paint here and a wipe over there.

The barn in the months leading up to the launch was a hive of activity. The final fit out seems to take forever. A perfectionist, it seemed to me, would never get his boat in the water.

However, some of the jobs, which I had grieved about not finishing – a shelf here and a cupboard there –, dwindled into insignificance when we launched. They may get done someday, they may not, and depending on how much their lack affects my comfort. It all seems so logical now.

I confess to a weakness for doing pleasant but inessential jobs and for this I have no regret. Having a few spare feet of iroko planking left over from making the rail I decided that *Ospray* would look very becoming wearing a pair of carved tailboards. Accordingly I doodled around on paper, then on cardboard cut outs which were taped in place and viewed from all angles before the jigsaw and chisel shaped timber into a sort of stylised osprey.

JOSHUA'S OLD JOANNA

One special job I have been hoarding until I have time to do it justice. My friend Lance Jackson inherited through a link only slightly less tenuous than my cat running across your back yard, a broken down piano which once belonged to none other than Mrs Joshua Slocum, though whether the first or the second I cannot tell. The carcass of this old Joanna, which for all I know may have had old Josh tapping his feet to many a lively tune, is veneered burr walnut which I reckon will make a fine drinks cabinet for the *Ospray* and may be a box for the ship's papers. What a remarkable stroke of luck! I could scarcely believe the coincidence and good fortune.

During the building of a boat, as Slocum found, doubting Thomas' abound. Eyes wide with naked doubt they ask *"will it float"* my reply to this was a withering sneer which I had practised in front of a mirror, to the point where I almost caused a heart attack to an old boy in the gents at the pub.

"How will you get it out of the barn", was another popular one, about which I had by own lurking doubts, thus causing me to develop techniques of evasiveness, which would have made a politician green with envy. That way you don't look such a Charlie if things go wrong.

To accomplish this tricky task, which involved a journey of only 200 feet but three sharp corners, Rob and I constructed a monstrous bogie from eight lorry wheels on two axels and 3 in. steel tubing, plus a few odds and ends of scaffolding. This was to move her to a concrete pad from which she would be fitted onto a low loader for her final journey to the sea.

The day finally came for *Ospray's* first move from the cosy barn where she had been hatched and reared. My feelings were mixed. I had the classic 'apron strings' syndrome of the worst of possessive parents.

Nevertheless the winch cables were shackled to the bogie and the tractor engine laboured under the strain of *Ospray's* bulk. Slowly she began to move like some vast antediluvian creature waddling from the swamp. As she emerged into the bright afternoon sunlight I was astonished when a skein of Canada geese, bugling merely, flew at tree top height over *Ospray's* bows. *"We're heading north"*, they seemed to clamour, and *"will you join us?"* I was rooted to the spot and forgot my camera hanging round my neck.

We had worked out a method by which we would lift her with six massive jacks whilst the wagon backed under her when she would be lowered into position. This was to save money. The minimum hire rate for a crane beefy enough to do the job was £200. However beware! Jacking up a 16-ton boat is even more tricky than it first appears and even though we had planned the job out, we almost came to grief. All went well until the wagon bed was within 5 ft of its final position. Then with a sickening crunch one of the jacks disappeared into the 3 ft diameter slice of tree trunk on which it stood.

The boat was eventually jacked into position again and safely loaded but the surliness of the transport people marred the day and the inevitable tension marred the occasion even before things went wrong. Anyone who cannot raise a smile on someone else's big day shouldn't be in this line of business. It's a bit like having a bad tempered old Vicar officiating at a wedding.

Ospray's 80-mile journey to the coast was something of a spectacle. Oak branches littered the decks as she burrowed through those leafy Welsh valleys and soared over mountain

Through the Welsh mountains to the sea.

passes, through the drifting tendrils of the mist, on the final triumphant journey to her natural element where she sat more like a fat complacent duck than a bird of prey. Throwing overboard those oak branches into the sea seemed somehow symbolic. A ritualistic severance of the last ties with the land.

Mum about to do the honours.

Dear old Mum poured the bubbly over the bows with the same intent thoroughness that she might clean the sink, leaving no crevice unsprayed. Suffice it to say I was speechless!

Ospray has found a cosy berth. She snuggles against the harbour wall surrounded by her big sisters. The trawlers and seiners and a friendly old tug. All the hubbub of a commercial harbour and it's very practical boat owners who have caused *Ospray* many a maidenly blush with their compliments but, much more have been unstinting with their advice to myself, the novice.

A friendly atmosphere pervades the place, fostered by the Harbour Master and his family who are themselves traditional boat enthusiasts.

Rigging ship was an affair, which extended over several weeks, what with all the welcome distractions of folk working up alongside for a 'gam', as Slocum put it, not that I got many retired whaling skippers, but I did get Will, a

In her berth at last.

retired boat builder, an expert once over for an insurance survey and pronounced her fit and well. Also a retired sail maker known in lyrical Wales, as Cale the Sail. The venerable Mr Cale was deeply appreciative of *Ospray's* bold lines and the beauty of her mainmast but was harshly critical of my gaff span, "*Carry away on a gale it will*", he lilted. Next week I arrived to find a hand spliced, very rugged, gaff span waiting to be fitted and my naked gaff saddle, leathered and tallowed, so softly that it wouldn't bruise a maiden's thigh let alone a hefty spruce mast for which he had displayed such affection.

Cale the Sail has taken *Ospray's* rigging under his wing, hoping I suspect to protect her from any amateurish blunder I might make. He hoped I wouldn't be offended at him having mentioned the weakness in my gaff span. I remarked that if it had to be a Welshman, who pointed out my error, I would rather it be he than Davy Jones Esq.

One thing would be very hard to have aboard a gaff rig boat would be too much rope. You seem to use miles of the stuff. Jimmy Green, Marine of the Coachyard, Beer in Devon apart from a well priced range of general yachting ropes do a range of three strand polyester ropes treated to look like natural hemp or tarred hemp. It looks great on traditional boats and I am just rigging a set of lazy jacks to gather *Ospray's* mainsail – still known as the muvver-in-law because of her exceedingly ample proportions. Heavy enough to command respect without having to get nasty as someone remarked about a Shire stallion, which had just stepped placidly on his foot.

The cloth of all the sails except the Genoa is 18oz Duradon, which I must confess, is a touch on the heavy side perhaps but not likely to blow away 'in a capful of wind'.

The blocks are almost all wooden ones, gleaned from Beaulieu and other boat jumbles. I bought some beauties with bronze roller bearings at the Northern Boat Jumble held at Liverpool in October. These events are becoming very popular and rightly so, one man's junk being another man's treasure. I must say I enjoy them immensely and meet many old friends with whom to exchange a few insults. Beaulieu, for sheer size will hold pride of place for a long time I imagine but who knows? A vast amount of gear changes hands at these venues including a lot of lovely old gear, which may otherwise never again have seen the light of day. In addition, is a lot of new stuff aimed at the sensible end of the market, making refreshing feet on the ground change from some modern chandlers where one is dazzled by the display and numbed by the price tag? It's a bit much when one has to re-mortgage the vessel before replacing the rigging screws.

Ospray's sea trials under engine only have begun and things are looking good, after an ignominious return from her first trip, being hauled home by the nose after her engine stalled and failed to restart due to a flat battery. This voyage, for which everyone except the village band had turned out, failed even to reach the harbour entrance. Oh, the embarrassment.

The next time we slid stealthily out, hardly anyone noticed, and all went perfectly. Well it would wouldn't it!

And away we went.

Chapter 10

The Keeper of the Morgue

Shortly after beginning work on *Ospray,* I was given a new title, which I would happily have done without. I became known to the local police force by the title – Keeper of the Morgue.

The barn in which I built *Ospray* was part of a farm belonging to Severn Trent Water Authority. It was decided by the powers that be, that there was a need for the temporary accommodation of 'Dirty Bodies'. This was the unflattering term for persons who had been found dead after a period, rendering the temporary storage likely to be distressing for anyone coming to identify a relative. So a stout wooden building was installed next to the barn in which *Ospray* was being built. The first guest arrived with police escort one night after dark. He was placed on the large lead slab, covered with a white sheet. The police departed leaving me to finish a final wipe down when a gust of wind blew the door shut with a loud bang! I came close to requiring new underwear. I had been very aware of the still figure under the sheet. I had never seen a dead person before and knew that I must do so if I was to fulfil my new responsibilities. When I pulled back the sheet I was amazed to feel only a profound sympathy for this poor old guy, who apparently was a tramp, and who often slept in barns on a cold night.

The pathologist whose job it was to determine the cause of death of our temporary guests was a cheery chap by the name of Henry. Henry was very methodical and began his examination by sticking his selection of scalpels in a neat line into the patient's thigh, whilst humming a merry tune. I was recounting my fright about when the door slammed shut.

Henry chuckled and said dryly, "These poor souls are long past harming anyone. It's the live buggers you have to watch out for on a dark night"!

A high brick wall separated the morgue from the adjacent lane, which was popular with horse riders. I began to notice that when we had a guest, there were some horses that refused point blank to pass.

My sons were naturally aware of the morgue and its purpose as one can imagine. Working late on a dark and windy night was fraught with possibilities for a vivid imagination: not to mention the occasional joke in very poor taste. On one such night, Mark was returning to the house from a small job he was doing on the boat, whilst I was on the way down to the barn. I saw him approaching in the dark and crouched behind a wall, grabbing his leg as he passed. To say he nearly went into orbit is an understatement! Needless to say, the joke was not repeated!

Chapter 11

Joshua's Journey
(From an article in BWee flight magazine.)

Almost 100 years ago, Captain Joshua Slocum, in his beloved little ship *Spray*, sailed through the West Indies at the end of an epic voyage of 46,000 miles. He was the first sailor to circum navigate the globe single-handed. He accomplished this feat in a vessel under 40 ft long and more than 90 years old, given to him in jest by an old whaling captain named Eben Pierce. The jest was that she was a total wreck, and Slocum had to rebuild her timber by timber.

However, the jest rebounded; for Slocum carved a place in maritime history for himself and the *Spray* with a feat, which many said, could not be done.

Joshua Slocum was a 'blue nose' Nova Scotian from a race whose self-reliance, hardiness and versatility are legendary. Born in 1844 he ran away to sea at the age of 12 after being thrashed for building a model ship instead of making sea boots in his father's workshop. He rose quickly through the ranks and at 18 was promoted to second mate, delighted at having come through the 'hawse pipe' and not through the 'cabin windows'.

Before he was 27 he was captain of the Washington, a magnificent square-rigged ship in which he sailed to Sydney, Australia, where he met and married his wife Virginia. Together they sailed the seven seas and enjoyed many years of adventure, he as a master of some of the finest vessels afloat, until sail began to be replaced by steam and Slocum found himself redundant; as he said 'cast up on the beach'. Unable to 'swallow the anchor', he let it be known that he was looking for a ship, which is where we meet old Eben

Pierce and his wreck. Slocum's voyage in this wreck took three years from 1895 to 1898 and his book about it, Sailing Alone Around the World, inspired me to build *Ospray*, a *Spray* look-alike, in which to follow in Slocum's wake.

An extract from Slocum's log, as he reaches the Caribbean. "Tonight in latitude 7 degrees 13 minutes north, for the first time in nearly three years, I see the north star". Two days later, "on the 20th May, about sunset, the island of Tobago off the Orinoco, came into view bearing west by north, distant 22 miles". The Spray was drawing rapidly towards her home destination; Boston, Massachusetts.

Later that night, running along the coast of Tobago Slocum was alarmed to find himself as he thought, amongst breakers. He lamented the day he had allowed on board a goat, which had eaten his charts of the West Indies. For hours heart in mouth, expecting to be wrecked at any moment he steered this way and that to clear the reefs he was sure surrounded him. Always he saw the flash of white water ahead.

At last, from the crest of a wave higher than the rest, he could see all there was to see of the reef and fell back speechless with amazement. "It was the great revolving light on the island of Trinidad, 30 miles away, throwing flashes over the waves which had deceived me".

He set course for Grenada, "a lovely island with people worth knowing", and cast anchor off the town of St Georges, 42 days sailing from the Cape of Good Hope. After giving a talk on his adventures to an audience in the courthouse, Slocum sailed for Dominica where he was boarded by a pompous custom official who was "starched from clew to earring and stood as straight up and down as a fathom of pump water". Then on to Antigua where the *Spray* was towed into St Johns harbour with some ceremony by a steam launch bearing Sir Frances Fleming, then governor of the Leeward Islands.

This was not Joshua Slocum's first visit to the West Indies. Ten years before, the bold captain had been ship wrecked on the coast of Brazil, where he lost his beautiful barque the *Aquidneck* with a cargo of timber, but saved his crew and his wife with their two boys. With only a few hand tools, the family built a 35 ft boat, which they aptly named the *Liberdade* to celebrate both their own freedom and that of the Brazilian slaves on May 13th, the day the family sailed for home via the West Indies.

"On the 19th day from Pernambuco, early in the morning we made out Barbados away in the west. First the blue fertile hills then the green fields came into view, studded with many white buildings between centuries of giant windmills. Barbados is the most pleasant island in the Antilles, to sail around its green fringe of coral is simply charming. We stood into the coast, sailing close so as to rake in a view of the whole delightful panorama. By noon we rounded the south point of the island and shot into Carlysle Bay".

The voyage for Brazil was not without incident. Garfield, the Slocum's youngest son declared, "Mammy this boat ain't big enough to pray in" after being thrown from his knees in heavy weather. On another occasion, a 60 ft whale surfaced under the boat, throwing it into the air. The family were at dinner at the time. With his usual masterly understatement, Slocum reports "the meal was finished without desert".

The Slocums were treated royally in Barbados but eventually, when the hurricane season was drawing to a close the *Liberdade* sailed for Puerto Rico. "The passage through the islands was magical! Fair breezes filled the sails of the Liberdade as we glided along over tranquil seas, scanning eagerly the islands as they came into view. The birds too, of rare plumage were there flying from island to island, the same as seen by the discoverers, and the sea with fishes teemed of every gorgeous hue, to lend enchantment to the picture and thrill the voyager now the same as then".

Slocum tells of a lad returning home with tales from the West Indies. "Mountains of sugar, rivers of rum and.. flying fish!" His mother chided him; "Don't lie to me John. Mountains of sugar no doubt you saw, and even rivers of rum, but flying fish there could never be!" The *Liberdade* sailed past Santa Cruz, which Slocum tagged "the island of brave women". Sailing through island scenery "worth the perils of ten voyages to see", the *Liberdade* reached Mayaguez, Puerto Rico, five days out from Barbados. "This was to be our last run among the trees of the West Indies and we made the most of it. Such a port for mariners I shall never see again. The port officials, kind and polite, extended all courtesies to the quaint barco pequina".

Having been gripped by these yarns of Slocum's ocean wanderings, is it any wonder that I was seized by a compulsion to own a boat and sail the seas as he had done?

Own a boat? Buying a 40 ft ocean goer was out of the question. I would have to build one, and it must be a *Spray*. Slocum's love for his brave little ship was contagious.

Naturally there were problems. One of these was my total lack of experience. Until then my principal achievements in the field of construction had been a coffee table with a wonky leg and a stone fireplace, which had been likened to the north face of the Eiger. However I did have some resources, a barn in which to build, and a son who was a welder. This last clinched my decision to build a copy of the *Spray* - in steel.

Thus began in the very heart of England, 80 miles from the sea, a 3½-year project. It started as a means to an end, but soon became an obsession, which governed all my waking hours, and many of my sleeping ones too. "It was my purpose to make my vessel stout and strong", wrote Slocum. These words rang in me ears as we hammered and forged 15 tons of steel into a rugged hull, which we fitted out with timber from trees that we had cut down ourselves.

They say that a boat is a hole in the water into which a man pours his money. To stem the ebb tide of my dwindling resources, I wrote articles for magazines, I catered for weddings, funerals and other joyous occasions, anything that would buy a gallon of paint or a pack of welding rods. All on top of a fulltime job. I read for at least two hours a day; my elevated platform of ignorance required every stage to be extensively researched.

This worked well; I ended up with a boat founded on many opinions rather than one.

I often imagined the wraith of Joshua Slocum hovering over us, nodding his grim approval as we worked to make her "stout and strong".

One summers night, weary with toil, I crept back down to the barn, unable to sleep without one last look at her. I gazed up at this majestic shape gleaming black in the darkness. She was finished!

The *Ospray* sailed to Ireland, Scotland and the misty Hebrides, Tir-nan-Og – the Land of the Ever Young. Wherever we cast anchor, folks recognise her for what she was and would row out to have a look at us. At the end of 1991, the *Spray* came again to Trinidad, to follow in Slocum's route through the Caribbean. The first rays of the sun threw into sharp relief the forested tops of the northern range; the *Ospray* battled a strong tide as we entered the Dragon's mouth. Frigate birds, pelicans and – believe it or not – an osprey wheeled over our little vessel. At a quarter to eight, after a voyage of over 5,000 miles from England along the ancient trade winds route, we dropped anchor in Harts Cut Bay.

We had visited Galicia, with its fabulous seafood, the volcanic isles of the Canaries with their stunning mountain scenery, their miles of concrete jungle and arid lunar landscape. We had called at the remote and weirdly beautiful Cape Verde Islands, where people smile all day long and swimmers wallop nosey hammerhead sharks on the nose to make them go away. Our voyage from the Cape Verdes to Trinidad had taken 21 days, with the northeast trades behind us. Apart from a few squalls at night, where terrifying black arches would engulf the boat in lashing rain and buffeting blasts of wind, the trip had been peaceful. Majestic Atlantic rollers urged the *Ospray* along, her 17 tons would be picked up bodily and we would surf down the face of the waves; shoals of flying fish scattered as we ploughed a furrow through the ocean towards a family Christmas in Trinidad.

Then, early in 1992 we set sail to follow in Joshua Slocum's wake, following the *Spray* through the islands. We had already seen flying fish; still to come perhaps, were the mountains of sugar and rivers of rum.

PART 2

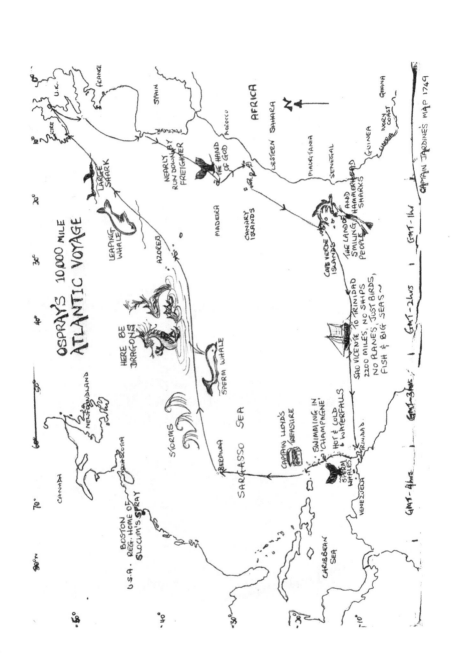

Chapter 1

The Beginning of the Voyage

"Let go forward", came the command, "let go aft". At last, we were off. Laden down to her marks with eleven hundred tea bags and over a ton of other assorted stores, *Ospray* nosed out of her berth at Port Penrhyn on the Welsh coast, outward bound for the West Indies.

From the grand old Brixham smack *Vigilance* moored astern of us, wafted the strains of *The Sailor's Farewell* played on a melodeon by one of the crew. On other vessels, bells clanged and whistles tooted whilst ashore among the crowd of family and friends could be discerned the odd tear stained cheek. Whether they were tears of sadness or relief, I cannot say. As for me, I was choked with emotion and could not say a word.

Ospray's crew were myself, Else with whom I had been planning the voyage for three years, Mark, my third son and Vanessa, Else's stepdaughter.

13th August. "We passed the Tuskar Rock light house off the south east tip of Ireland in the early hours. With the spring tide under us, we were doing 9.3 knots. Three of us were feeling slightly unwell and one of us extremely unwell."

Poor Vanessa, she looked as though she had been carved out of ivory and retched constantly. The second morning dawned bright and clear with a vigorous chop in which *Ospray* rolled enthusiastically. The sink discharge pipe in the heads came adrift about 01.00 causing sea water to gush in with each roll. Else and Mark lifted the floorboards and baled it out which is just what you need on a queasy stomach. The skipper was of course involved in important ships duties! Toast and marmalade was adequate for breakfast. Unfortunately, marmalade did nothing to dispel Vanessa's *Mer-malade* as it is supposed to, according to Mary Queen of Scots.

We passed quite a few trawlers during the day working the rich Norway prawn grounds between Ireland and Wales. Myriads of gulls clamoured behind the trawlers as they hauled nets and a squadron of gannets patrolled two hundred feet above. Suddenly, the two left hand birds of the formation peeled off and with wings folded like the fletching on an arrow, went into a vertical dive. With urgency borne of panic, a hole appeared in the mass of squabbling gulls. Obviously one gives a diving gannet plenty of room.

The Isles of Scilly lay more or less on our course, so we decided to call in at Hughtown, St Mary's to top up with fuel. The approach to Hughtown, it seems, was designed by the Almighty as an obstacle course for the mariner. Unbuoyed rocks and ledges conspire with shoals and strong cross-tides to ensnare the sailor. Their success over the centuries makes for sobering reading. Thinking that a crash into Hangman's island in the middle of the night at such an early stage in the voyage might depress the crew and possibly diminish their faith in the skipper, I ordered a reduction in speed to ensure our arrival in daylight.

Else woke me with a cup of tea at 06.00 and I came on deck to find Mark at the wheel and the Scilly Isles spread in front of us like carelessly dropped pieces of jigsaw puzzle. To my relief, I saw a French yacht ahead of us and for a while we tagged along in her wake. My relief evapourated instantly when the Frenchman suddenly veered to port and describing a tight curve came round to follow in *Ospray's* wake. I said nothing but hitched up the Union Jack another foot.

Mark did a brilliant pilotage job doing everything strictly by the book and we came to anchor in Hughtown harbour at about 08.30. By the time we had tidied up and gone ashore my knuckles had resumed their normal colour and we were ready for a big breakfast. Except for poor Vanessa, who viewed her piece of toast as she ate it, I thought, with the cynical distaste of someone confident of viewing it a gain before long. However, within an hour, she began to look less like a recent exhumation and once more began to regard death as something to be avoided rather than welcomed as a friend.

The Scillies are delightfully Olde Worlde. Painted houses huddle round tiny harbours stacked high with lobster pots and bestrewn with nets being mended or drying in the sun. All too soon, it was time to refuel and catch the tide south for Biscay which we hoped, one of us more fervently than the others, would not live up to its boisterous reputation. However, Vanessa was soon to have yet another small sum of misery added to the foot of her account!

Due to a misunderstanding with the pumps operator, the fuel tank overflowed over the water tanks and into the bilges and, despite an intensive clean up, into the water tanks. The smell of diesel hung about for days. Now an oily smell is a well known catalyst for a queasy tum and we had hardly set sail before the poor lass was embracing the bucket and calling for Hughie.

As we cleared the Scillies in calm sunny weather, we encountered the swell of the Atlantic, rising and falling like the chest of a sleeping giant. I gazed through the binoculars at the great Wingletang rock, which I thought must have been named by Edward Lear.

Else made a vegetable bake at Mark's request with broccoli, carrots, cauliflower and courgettes with eggs and a cheese sauce full of spices. Chelsea buns and doughnuts were for afters. Vanessa was in temporary possession of a cup of hot chocolate.

The first night out from the Scillies put us in the Western Approaches to the English Channel. The navigation lights of several ships could be seen at any time demanding extreme vigilance. Passing some seventy miles west of Ushant, we were glad to be clearing the busy shipping lanes of this area.

The next day was clear and bright with a steady breeze from the north east of about force four. *Ospray* ambled contentedly along under full main and genoa. The world seemed a fine place, vibrant with the excitement of unknown prospects. What sights should we see? What dangers and challenges would we face? How would we cope, as individuals and as a team? How would *Ospray* stand up to the rigours of a multi thousand-mile voyage? I had tried to emulate Slocum who wrote regarding the building of his beloved *Spray*, *"It was my purpose to make my vessel stout and strong"*.

Whenever faced with a choice in her construction, I had always opted for the stronger even though it often meant being heavier and usually more expensive. However, as the West Indians say, *"cheap ting no good and good ting no cheap"*.

We were now entering with just a little trepidation the notorious Bay of Biscay, which was not living up to its

Bones of the Spray.

Timber!

Mainmast.

Loaded up ready for off!

Up the lane in a cloud of dust.

Jim at Bangor.

boisterous reputation. However, the wise man counts not his chickens until they are hatched and we listened to each shipping forecast with more than casual interest, breathing a communal sigh of relief at the continued absence of gale warnings while each feigned indifference to the others. Each movement of the barometer was subjected to intense scrutiny and suspicion, minding me of the *"Duke of Marlborough who, trusting the slight rise in the glass had prepared for a day's fishing. The story goes that His Grace flung the unfortunate instrument out into the pouring rain exhorting it, in lurid terms, to go and see for itself."*

Towards evening a large school of dolphins exploded over the horizon and joined *Ospray* romping and leaping alongside for an hour in a spree of jubilation. Impish smiles on their faces like a bunch of kids let out of school and bent on mischief. After they left us for less boring companions, we sailed down the moonbeam for several hours but never reached the moon. The peace was broken only by the occasional dull boom from the big mainsail and the sound of Vanessa retching into her bucket which had become her constant companion. We christened her rent-a-snack because whatever she ate was very speedily returned. Sometimes apparently, with interest.

Later that night a stiffish breeze sprang up from the north east which, conflicting with the westerly swell, caused an awkward lop with the occasional big lump which caught *Ospray* by surprise. Mark said that at one stage his bunk in the vulnerable fo'castle dropped away from under him leaving him in a temporary state of levitation. Shortly after this mildly alarming event he was doing his best to nod off when *Ospray* struck a rather peevish sea at an odd angle. *Berdoof*, sending a cascade of spray over the bow. Unfortunately, Mark had left the forward hatch open through which he had been counting the stars instead of sheep hoping thereby to induce slumber. A middle-sized dollop of the cold Atlantic struck him full in the face. My view from the cockpit of a bedraggled naked figure swearing fluently as he slammed the hatch closed brought to mind Ernest Shackleton's silent rage during the epic voyage of the tiny *James Caird* in the Atlantic Ocean. Shackleton had just crawled from his comfortless wet bed on the rock ballast of the boat, when on sticking his head over the tarpaulin cover he received a quart of sub zero southern ocean down his neck. Said the mate on watch, trying not to laugh, *"Bit juicy tonight, Sir"*.

On the next routine check of the engine, I found that a connecting hose had split and seawater was cascading over the alternator, which amazingly was still belting out 25 amps. Having switched off the engine, I did a quick repair to the hose. Quick repairs are not noted for longevity and this was no exception. Within two hours we had once more a water-cooled alternator. This time I made a better job using a piece of Else's skirt (discarded), a generous slathering of silicone rubber topped off with three polythene bags with the bottoms cut off and taped on with self amalgamating rubber tape. With devilish cunning I kept in reserve a sleeve from an old oilskin jacket. This time I left the compound to go off overnight. The repair lasted until I fitted a new hose flown out at great expense by Lancing Marine of Brighton to Vigo in Spain. It was necessary to run the engine several hours a day to keep the batteries charged. The main drain on which was the auto pilot. Steering a boat can be quite romantic and is fine and dandy for a few hours. However, Henry (the Navigator) our mechanical helmsman was an absolute boon. He did not eat, sleep, rest or drink yet he generously allowed other members of the crew to get on with important duties such as reefing or making a brew or going for a nap. When he occasionally broke down, panic prevailed until a team of eager but clueless surgeons and nurses diagnosed his problem and made him well again. Dear old Henry, what would we have done without him. Get well soon Henry. Please.

17th August. 23.55 log entry. *"Romping along in fine style but has the bit between her teeth. Put a reef in the main and she handles much easier".*

In the early hours of the 19th, we were doing around seven and a half knots, which is good work for *Ospray*. We were under sail and unable to start the engine due to the recent hose repair. Else radioed a big cargo vessel, which seemed to be bearing down on us from the NNE. The radio operator was Polish. Now Else can make a stab at one or two languages but Polish is not one of them. Having spent several minutes trying but failing to find a common denominator, the ship was noticeably closer and still on course for *Ospray*. The Pole meanwhile was obviously enjoying practising his very sparse English on a lady and roaring with laughter every time she mentioned collision. Else, anxious not to convey any hint of unseamanly panic, passed the time of day pleasantly and asked politely if it was not too much trouble, would they mind steering just a weenie bit to the west thinking to save the inconvenience of an eighty mile swim to the nearest beach.

However, after commenting on such trifles as the appalling price of Vodka, he must have noticed that Else's voice, though still steady and coherent, had risen by half an octave or maybe he could hear me screaming invectives from the cockpit for I saw the geometry of his lights suddenly alter. The green swing away from the red and the vessel slid past us into the darkness. The Pole still chattering away to ease the loneliness of his radio vigil. I remarked to Else, slightly testily I think, that I was glad it was not a long distance 'phone call with me paying the bill.

Towards evening we jibed. The boom vang snapped and as the mainsail lashed over, two reef points tore out and ripped the sail quite badly. So, closing the door securely behind the bolting horse we put in another reef. *Ospray* immediately became docile and handled beautifully. What was it that my father said? "Do it now!"

19th August. "Now approaching Cape Finnisterre. Engine back on to charge the batteries and no leaks from the repaired hose. Big seas running, one or two quite awesome but Ospray riding them like a swan".

In the greyness of dawn, I was on the helm and happened to look down the hatchway to see Vanessa peering from her bunk. Dark brown eyes huge in a pale face. I raised my hand and she managed the ghost of a smile. Then, if possible, her eyes widened even more and I glanced over my shoulder to see the rearing shape of a huge wave, black and menacing in the half-light. I saw it begin to topple, like a stricken giant, then with a tremendous roar it broke in a welter of foam as it passed our stern. *Ospray* never even staggered but sailed grandly on as though she was bred to cope with such trifles, which indeed she was.

Many sailors have remarked how well she handles big following seas without the yawing and threat of broaching which many vessels display. I was glad we had put in a second reef earlier.

> It was,   *Like one that on a lonesome road,*
> *Doth walk in fear and dread,*
> *And having once turned round walks on,*
> *And turns no more his head;*
> *Because he knows a frightful fiend*
> *Doth close behind him tread.*

Not long after this the engine cut out. I found the problem was due to a blockage in the fuel line which I eventually cleared by sucking in mouthfuls of diesel and spitting it into a bucket until I sucked out the blockage which was a shiny piece of something or other which even now I prefer not to think too much about. It was fearfully hot in the engine room. That and the plunging of the ship and some speculation as to the nature of the blockage caused me to retch enthusiastically. This did little to settle Vanessa's stomach and soon the boat was filled with a cacophony of violent heaves each vying with the other in urgency summoning Hughie and Ralph.

Life seemed a little better when we got into the lee of Cape Finnisterre out of the north easterlies, which were now blowing quite strongly. We entered the Ria de Muros and by 18.30 were dropping anchor in fifty feet of glass calm water just off the little town of Muros. After making all snug, we rowed ashore and went for a stroll which served the purpose of searching out the best buy in terms of a meal and to give Vanessa a chance to practise walking on land which she said at first seemed to move more than the sea. Having found a likely taverna from which wafted appetising smells, a charcoal grill in full production, Mark and I ordered fish that turned out to be albacore. Vanessa wearily ordered a steak whilst Else fancied a large steak. Unfortunately there seemed to be a language problem, which for some time remained unresolved. I knew the Spanish for fish so that was okay. Coca-cola is universal but Else could not remember the Spanish for steak. However, Else is nothing if not resourceful and after a few mock charges up and down the taverna floor with two fingers pointing from lowered forehead and cries of "el toro" alternating with "tum te tum te tum te tum" representing the tattoo of hooves on some baked earth, a faint light of understanding gleamed in the waitress's eyes. We were not to know it then but the Galicians are not noted for frivolity.

Next day after bacon and eggs for breakfast, we all went ashore to explore Muros, which is a charming little fishing village with numerous outside bistros serving all manner of seafood displayed in the most tantalising fashion. The town is set amongst hills which have the look of Greece about them. We bought peaches and pears from the outside fruit market, which I thought tasted sort of foreign. Probably just different varieties.

On the waters of the Ria off the town bustled all manner of fishing boats, many were dories of ten to twelve feet long and beautifully painted in the brightest of colours. Fishing is in the blood of the Galician who regards a minute not to spend fishing as a minute wasted.

That night we were treated to a spectacle. On a tall pedestal set up in the main square, a musician had installed a performing goat. The goat's job was to dance on the tiny top of the pedestal accompanied by a tune played on the musician's trumpet, the stridency of which would have woken Pancho Villa from his slumbers in the grave. Every time the goat stopped dancing, the musician smote the goat a hearty blow with his trumpet, which was supposed to instil enthusiasm, but only served to harden the look of resigned desolation in the poor creatures eyes, but drew a few more coins from the sympathetic onlookers. During the whole performance and long afterwards, a dog howled dismally in a nearby street, though whether this was from pain, loneliness or the sound of the trumpet, I can only hazard a guess.

Ham, potatoes, carrots and cabbage were for supper followed by a slice of fruitcake.

Inspired by the diligence of the local Pescadores, I fished for a couple of hours after supper using mussel and ham skin for bait. I caught two fish each of about two ounces. One of which was so repulsive as to constitute a cast iron defence against any sighted creature and against even an unsighted one with a shred of imagination.

A large old ketch with a wishbone rig came in about 09.00 and at the second attempt anchored about one cable away. At almost the same time as the anchor hit the water from the bow, the dinghy splashed down astern and the crew, who seemed to be English, leaped aboard and rowed lustily for the taverna on the shore. The wind had increased slightly so I veered more cable before turning in with a glass of wine and R. L. Stevenson's 'Kidnapped'. Even better the second time round by the light of an oil lamp and the creak of the vessel in the gathering breeze.

About two in the morning, Vanessa woke us to tell us that there was a ship alongside. Supposing that we had dragged anchor, we leapt out of bed stark naked to find the old ketch had dragged her anchor, which had probably never bitten the bottom and she had bumped us. Her crew in various states of undress and befuddlement were running round like headless chickens stubbing their toes whilst being berated by the skipper. Eventually they sorted themselves out and re-anchored some distance away.

We were up not too early in the morning and after a quick row ashore for fresh bread, we heaved anchor and set a course for Puebla del Cariminal in the next Ria. However a stiff breeze in our teeth reduced speed to a bumpy two knots, so after an hour we turned back for Muros. The day was windy with rain and squalls of some violence would rattle the boat every hour or so. Throughout all this a dory man sat steadily jigging away catching every so often some tiny creature, which went into his bucket. For every pescado, he lit up another fag, which smouldered away protected slightly from the downpour by the brim of his hat. Whether the day resulted in a credit or a debit would be hard to say but it seems the Galician must fish. He does not, however, smile a great deal. Our beaming "buenos dias" would be greeted with a penetrating stare.

We later went shopping in a supermercado where I had a strong fancy for a loaf shaped like a lavatory seat thinking that I might never have the chance again. However, Else chose two loaves bearing no resemblance whatsoever to lavatory seats at which I felt quite unaccountably miffed, vowing to return and buy up the whole stock of lavatory seat shaped loaves if only to establish my 'droit de seigneur' as skipper of the ship!

The 30-mile trip to Puebla del Cariminal was uneventful except for our outrage at seeing a trawler dumping a dozen large plastic sacks of rubbish over the side in the beautiful Ria de Arosa. Environmental awareness is late in coming to this lovely area.

Puebla del Cariminal is delightful. A wonderful huddle of red buildings teeming with tavernas and cafes. Here and there are tiny squares usually dominated by a church or a public building ornamented by exquisite sculptures often with the theme of fishing which is the 'raison d'etre' of the village whose name means village of the dories. Mark departed by coach to meet his friend at Vigo airport.

From the beginning of the voyage, and even before, Mark had been prevailing upon me to allow his best friend Sean to come along. A notion which, until now, I had resisted. Partly because I am particularly choosey with whom I spend long periods cooped up in a boat and Sean was something of an unknown quarter. Also, the last time I had seen Sean was when he and Mark were at college together and they were both going through a rebellious phase of carefully cultivated scruffiness which seemed to have succeeded beyond their wildest dreams and from which Mark has never quite emerged. I had visions of these two in their appalling shreds and tatters being a magnet for every customs official in the world.

However, I need not have worried. Sean turned up shy and shiny clean in an unriven shirt and modest khaki shorts without a single gash or tear, which became known as Sean's 'old colonials'. He immediately fitted in with the ship's company and soon became a much loved and valuable crewmember.

Vanessa established a good rapport with the two lads and there was much good-natured leg pulling. She was feeling much better now we were in Vigo after being chronically sick each time we went to sea. She and Else and I formed the 'three musketeers' and went everywhere together on land whilst the two boys went off on their own.

Vigo is a beautiful, cultured city, with cool tree lined avenues and everywhere are sculptures of beasts or groups of people. The buildings are decorated with the most incredibly ornate ironwork that must have cost the earth even a century ago. We went a long walk to the castle high on the hill and passed a pathetic little dog who had crept into a crevice in the rock and died. We felt very sad and thought of two little friends at home. Everywhere were tavernas with mouth watering displays of seafood in the windows. Large tanks with live lobsters and langoustines were all quite expensive.

We had ordered some spares for the engine to arrive at Vigo airport, so Mark and Sean after a whole morning filling in forms at the Customs office eventually zoomed off to the airport and after a long but half-hearted search and many Gallic shrugs by the airport officials, the parts were found and brought back to the boat.

Dealing with officialdom, banks etc. is a nightmare in Spain. Everything takes forever and the service is rarely cheerful but here and there one comes across a little oasis of friendliness, which makes it all worthwhile.

At 06.30 we cast off our moorings and motored down the Ria, there being no wind, and after two hours dropped anchor in the bay at Bayona. It was a fine sandy bottom and after the usual kick astern we felt *Ospray* tremble slightly as the anchor buried itself and we knew we were safe for that night. Bayona is a quaint old town dominated by a magnificent castle and a huge statue of the Virgin Mary watching over the fishermen as they go out to earn their living on the capricious deep. After a few glasses of vino and a plate of squid in a taverna, we wandered round a street market where vendors of all nationalities were displaying their wares. We were riveted by a gorgeous Peruvian rug into which designs of llamas had been woven. After a good deal of haggling we secured this prize for 20,000 pesetas which was all the three of us musketeers had on us. So back to the boat.

The boys had gone off with some Galician friends for the night to buy vino in the hills, so we three sat up on deck till the early hours sipping wine in the warm night air and listening to *Ospray* stirring gently at her chain whilst other yachts of all nationalities moored nearby stirred gently at their chains like sleepy horses in a stable.

A quarter moon hung over the brooding castle and the air was pregnant with the subdued excitement of the prospect of travel. We gazed at the other boats and the cosy glow of oil lamps through their portholes. We listened to the idle chatter carrying clear across the water and we pondered on the sights they had seen and the sights we had yet to see on our wanderings. And so to bed. At peace with the world.

Next morning after a late breakfast of boiled eggs, Vanessa quite well and eating heartily, we were off in the dingy to explore the town. Bayona is a painter's paradise with little alleys paved with large stones in warm mellow colours. The churches though had a cold austere look about them, possibly more feared than revered. Back to the boat about 14.00 intending to fish but fell asleep instead. When in Rome.... I woke up to find Else changing, standing naked with her back to me. I lay watching her for a while wishing we were alone. My reverie was disturbed by a knock on the hull, and a moustachioed face peering through the porthole, which took me by surprise, as we were half a mile from land. It was the harbour master in his launch collecting dues for anchoring in the bay which I have never known elsewhere. 400 pesetas for a night and a free 'what the butler saw' to boot. Else was a bit sniffy about this but could not find the right Spanish to tell him off.

The boys had returned from their quest for wine gleefully laden with several unlabelled bottles of wine and one of some kind of spirit. All at an astonishingly low price. We soon discovered why. I am not noted for my fussiness with regard to wine but this was so dreadful that it came close to being undrinkable. It was only regard for the lads' feelings that I forced it down. The spirit bottle bore no name but I suggested it could have been made by Molotov. One sip deprived me of speech and respiratory function for some time. Just as we were getting ready for bed a violent thunderstorm erupted around us with almost continuous lightening.

Next morning, 30th August, we were invited aboard *Papillon* a lovely green ketch, by skipper Tom and his wife D.L. who from our vantage point a couple of cable lengths away, seemed to spend much of her time aloft while Tom winched the bosun's chair and shouted instructions from the deck. I commended this arrangement to Else without any noticeable result. This doughty couple had sailed *Papillon* 40,000 miles before deciding to install an engine. We were treated to coffee and cake while Tom went through the charts of the West Indies up to the coast of the U.S. giving suggestions on pilotage, what to see and what to miss etc. Then D.L. took Else shopping to show her where to find the best buys. Tom and D.L. had been sailing *Papillon* for nearly 18 years and usually had one or two paying crewmembers at £60 per head per week. Else quizzed her about the crew rulebook and watch systems, some of which sound a good idea for *Ospray*.

Back on board *Ospray*, I tried the engine to make sure all was charged up and okay for tomorrow and our departure for Madeira. There was a loud clonk when I turned the key, then a laboured wheezing as she turned over. A few quick checks revealed water in the oil sump. Had she hydraulicked (sucked water back through the cooling system) or blown a gasket? We went ashore to try to locate expert help and eventually located a marine mechanic who had worked in a factory in England for some time and spoke English liberally bespattered with swear words which I think he thought were part of structured English. However, he confirmed that the ******* cylinder head gasket was okay and I wondered how he would describe it, had it not been okay. We diagnosed, by taste that the water in the oil sump was ******* seawater which rendered it likely that water had been sucked back through the system when the engine was switched off. I drained the sump, refilled with oil and ran the engine for two hours. No water. After that we released the vacuum on the water intake each time the engine was switched off. We have to stay till Monday to get money to pay Manuel, the mechanic.

1st September. – "Baking session on board Ospray. Cakes, mince pies and jam tarts made with home made blackcurrant jam".

The aroma must have drifted down wind as we soon had visitors. First Tom, D.L. and Lisa from Papillon, then Dave from Teal. Dave was an ex merchant seaman who had navigated with a road map from England having spent all his discharge money on his boat. His mainsail had a large tear, which Dave had left un-repaired so that he could better see where he was going. His inflatable dinghy was made in Taiwan and bore a prominent notice advising against exposure to sunlight. Dave got over this problem by inflating and deflating it every trip to shore which I thought may get tedious on a busy day. However, Dave was eternally cheerful and bubbled with enthusiasm when I asked him why he had swapped a well-paid life at sea, for an unpaid life at sea. He said, that for all the world you see in the Merchant Navy, you may as well walk round on an atlas. He often voyaged half way across the world, discharged the oil cargo into a terminal from which land was only a blur, then voyaged back again. He was of a mind to go to the West Indies but said if the wind did not seem quite right he would bear left and go to Cape Town, which would suit him just as well. He also said that he believed in having eight hours sleep every night and took his sails down from 22.00 hours till 08.00. We often wonder where he ended up and worried about him being run down twixt ten and eight.

Later we went to see the Virgin on the Rock. An immense statue carved from sandstone blocks overlooking the harbour. The Blessed Lady cradled a fishing boat in her arms and I made a silent prayer that maybe *Ospray* could be included in her protection. I think she will.

We found a very Spanish taverna with huge wooden casks larger than hogsheads and cured hams hanging everywhere. The wine was served in bowls and was extremely robust and deep dark red, which stained our mouths and tongues causing much mirth. Later, Vanessa insisted on treating me to a hock as I was drooling over each one that went past us to another table. Else shared it with me and it was scrumptious beyond belief served with a plate full of fried pimentos, some of which were real scorchers.

2nd September. "Last walk round town buying groceries and obtaining money for Manuel who, when found, resolutely refused to accept any payment for all his trouble. 'Next time you come we have a drink eh?' Bless his heart".

At 14.00, after saying goodbye to all our friends, we hove anchor and let the sails draw for Madeira nearly 800 miles distant. Following a powwow and notes gleaned from *Papillon,* we now set a watch system as follows using two hour rolling watches. Five crew, one crew on, three off and one on standby with the standby watch preceding your two hours on. Standby to cook the meal and clear away. This worked better than the old system, which followed the rule that 'he who cooks does not wash up'. Now this may seem fair but Mark, in particular, made such an horrendous mess when he cooked, using every receptacle in the ship, that volunteers to clear and wash up after him were unlikely to get killed in the rush. Also the standby at sundown had the honour of inventing a cocktail to celebrate another days voyaging. Some, as may be expected, were quite incendiary, many were very pleasant and the occasional one was memorable. Ospray Sundowner especially so.

Late afternoon we passed a trawler hauling her nets when a large shark swam past us in a leisurely fashion less than ten yards from the boat. Vanessa tried valiantly to cook a meal but retched constantly, which did little to sharpen my appetite. In the end Else came to her assistance and a meal was duly served.

In the early hours around 05.00 during Else's watch, the ship hit a drifting net, which wrapped round the prop while under engine and stopping the motor instantly. Nothing to be done until daylight, so the crew were sent back to bed while the vessel sailed herself, dead on course. The first mate treated the skipper to a little something special on deck while the boat rolled heavily in the swell.

September 3rd dawned with a dreary sky and a lumpy sea, which tossed the boat about reducing my relish for diving under the stern to around zero. Memories of yesterday's shark were still fresh in my mind and to make matters worse, as I stood on the afterdeck peering gloomily into the water a large shoal of little fish fled past the boat helter skelter, leaping out of the water in a mad panic. From what were they fleeing? My imagination demanded to know and immediately supplied the answer in the form of something with a faceful of sharp teeth. Nevertheless, on with the wet suit and over the side with on site support from Sean and Mark in the dinghy. Else stood on the stern and had one end of a rope, the other being tied around me for safety. Dipping my head below the stern, which was rising and falling with some vigour and threatening to brain me, there was the net trailing from the screw and below me were several miles of the most vivid indigo. The net was compacted into a solid mass and the only way was to dive the few feet to the screw, saw away with the knife, come up for air and repeat until the job was done. The whole time my head was swivelling like a radar scanner and I slashed my left hand quite badly with the knife. As I watched the blood streaming away, my imagination went into overdrive and it was with only faint regret that having finished the task, I was heaved into the dinghy like a harpooned seal.

We sailed the rest of the day under full canvas and a light breeze on the starboard beam. About 01.00 on September 4th, the alternator packed up, so all lights and instruments were doused. The paraffin running lamps were lit in the shrouds and Henry the autopilot was given a night off to conserve battery power. Next morning, I installed the spare alternator.

Despite the accomplishments of all the ancient mariners who voyaged before engines were invented, this ancient mariner found the prospect daunting. Having a commercial engine such as our six cylinder Ford, we could carry a spare part for all the likely failures for a bearable outlay so we had plundered all the local scrap yards for serviceable parts. We had a starter motor, alternator, fuel pump, belts and filters and all manner of bits. All this weighed quite a lot but the peace of mind was worth the freightage.

Vanessa did her first night watch and Mark got up for two hours to support her, which pleased me. There was quite a rapport developing between the three young members of the crew and the presence of a young female probably had a stabilizing effect. There was a good deal of banter which kept a lively feel to the ship. *"Baked three loaves of bread rich in seeds and oatmeal and had a slice hot and dripping with butter and Marmite. Autopilot failed but worked after I fiddled with it. Heaven knows why"*. Mark made Korma curry for dinner, which went down well with a glass of beer.

For the next few days, the wind remained light so we motor sailed again and by sundown on September 6th, we had fuel enough for only fifteen hours, some of which we would need to get into port. By this time we were settling into a delightful routine of life at sea. The nights were warm and velvety black so that the constellations stood out like diamond necklaces. Progress was leisurely to slow and the days ran into each other very comfortably.

Due to the shortage of fuel, we reduced the engine use to two hours a day to keep the batteries charged. Steering was mostly by hand and at night we steered by a star, picking one which stood on our course. This is much easier than staring at a compass. And much more romantic.

Several schools of tuna followed us over the next few days, sometimes breaking off for a feeding frenzy on some dense shoals of small fish. They did not however get very frenzied about the numerous baits that I threw at them and so I tried a shot with the spear gun but missed, which pleased Mark no end. The only interruption in this tranquil passage was on the night of September 10th, when we sailed over the Seine Seamount which is more like an alp twenty miles across, soaring up from sixteen thousand feet to one hundred and eighty feet from the surface. The sea suddenly became very confused with sinister heavings and swirlings. At the same time a violent electrical storm erupted and rain lashed down for five hours. Lightning flashed almost continuously, for all the world like a colossal battle of heavy artillery. Sean said it was like sailing into Hades and he abandoned all hope of coming through alive. Imaginations flourished regarding the fearsome creatures which undoubtedly dwelt on the crags beneath the swirling waters. Shortly after the storm, Mark dashed down the steps into the engine room to start the engine. *"Can't stop now"*, he blurted. Next thing I felt the boat heel sharply and I clambered on deck to see a huge, rusty cliff ablaze with lights sweeping past at twenty-eight knots only a hundred yards away. Apparently the boys had seen the ship a long way off and tried radioing her, then flashing lights on our sails, then on her bridge and finally desperate evasive action only in the nick of time. Well done lads.

The next day, however, dawned peacefully to the most exquisite sunrise with clouds contorting themselves into fantastic shapes of lions and dragons, one becoming the other before our very eyes. The sea was the most incredible indigo blue and in the heat of the day, we trailed a rope over the side and leaped overboard for a swim or hung on the

"OH, THE BOCA AT DAYBREAK,
HOW CAN ONE DESCRIBE
THAT SCENE?
THE LITTLE EMERALD ISLANDS,
WITH THE SAPHIRE
SEA BETWEEN"

ENTRANCE TO THE
BOCAS IN TRINIDAD

rope like a trail of jellyfish. The vessel sailed herself doing barely half a knot. After a jolly half hour, a coil of rope twisted and nudged me in the back giving my imagination a jump-start which prompted our return to the ship. We launched the dinghy to get some pictures of *Ospray* who now sported a flying jib, which we rigged on an extension to the bowsprit to coax a shade more speed from her. *Ospray* looks superb and a little rakish and quite the ocean lady.

Again the days merged gently one into another. Land based life seemed in the distant past and voyaging became an end in itself. Early one morning, just before dawn, I was on watch with Vanessa, when she pointed out a bright light on the eastern horizon, which seemed to be rapidly approaching. I dived down below to radio the vessel which seemed to be on a collision course, then clattered back up the companionway steps to check her position. I could have died with embarrassment when I realized that it was not a masthead light but Venus.

Our progress is painfully slow due to constant lack of wind. We have plenty of food but most of the fresh fruit and veg and all of the meat have gone. We already fantasize about what we will eat when we reach land.

"Thick sizzling steaks with a crisp dewy salad and tangy tomatoes with a sprinkling of basil. Pints of ice cold lager with hops bursting out of every bubble says my diary for September 12th".

Just after midnight on my watch, I was musing about food as usual under a brilliant starry sky, when there was a vast sigh from right by the stern. Another one followed shortly after with the sound of water rushing over some great bulk. "Whale" I shouted. Heads erupted from every hatch like prairie dogs. We could hear the whale blowing now some distance from the vessel but it was too dark to see. Else came on deck next morning for her watch to find Sean reading and looking up she saw that we were surrounded by a pod of whales spouting round us. The minke whales gradually swam off over the next half hour. But a huge beast some two miles away, which we thought was a humpback or a sei, could still be seen when he went over the horizon. Everyone was thrilled to bits of course.

Because of the flying jib up forward, there is an imbalance in the sail plan and even with the helm hard to weather; we cannot hold our chosen course. After a little experimenting, Mark and I rigged up the stormsail on the back end of the big gaff mainsail lashed to an extension boom. This looked very Heath Robinson but gave us thirty degrees to starboard and dead on course.

I had been under some pressure from the boys to turn east and head for Casablanca. They were vying with each other for the best Humphrey Bogart with Peter Laurie impressions. Sean just had the edge with his Peter Laurie, *"I have a brother, he can get anything ...... anything"*. The boys often shared their watches and we could not help but hear some weird conversations.

Mark to Sean (who was trying to read), *"Sean, why is it that you have brown hair and yet your beard always comes out red?"*

Sean, (slightly testily) *"Oh, how on earth should I know? It just does"*.

Mark. *"You know what I reckon?"*

Sean, (grumpily), *"What do you reckon?"*

Mark. *"I reckon God just got absent minded and put his hand in the wrong chin box"*. Sean was silent and stared in disbelief.

13th September. At precisely four o'clock Vanessa shouted "Land". No doubt, she was looking harder than anyone else. Sure enough, fine on the starboard bow was the faintish of outlines, the four peaks of Porto Santo. Everyone was delighted except Vanessa who was ecstatic. Mark was chef for dinner and once more the recipe was based on beans, which we put down to a subconscious quest for more wind. The chilli, 'sans carne' with spicy popadums, was followed by sponge pudding with custard and the rest of the lager to celebrate sighting land. Our speed was down below one knot and still thirty miles to go. Women have a peculiar idea of priorities and I was presented with a request for some of our diminished water for hair washing. Not wishing to undermine confidence in our early landfall, I accepted with hardly a growl. The thought of nearly two days more in sight of land was unbearable, so I started the engine for a couple of hours hoping to get into the onshore winds which should blow near the island. We could now see Madeira but her peaks were still shrouded in cloud. Away to the south was Isla Deserta Grande, which is the last refuge of the Monks seal, and Isla Cao (Dog Island).

Chapter 2

The start of the Atlantic Islands

Our ploy seemed to work as we picked up a nice little breeze, which wafted us into Machico where we dropped anchor at about 20.00 on the 14th September.

Hungry for fresh sights, sounds and tastes, all hands were soon hauling the dinghy up the beach clear of the surf. The first thing of note we saw was a large rat by a stream on the beach. However, things improved rapidly and we were soon walking by groves of bananas and mangoes. Up on the steep terraces one could see corn on the cob and other food crops, not an inch of ground being wasted.

Machico is very pretty with the streets paved with cobbles laid in patterns. The ground rises steeply in terraces, around the town, to craggy peaks. Red tiled roofs bespeckle the hillsides. We found a shop and bought groceries, wine and cigarettes for our nicotine starved crew who fell on the fags like wolves. Madeira is a Portuguese island and hoping to impress the crew, in very broken Spanish and gestures, I enquired as to whether they were open, manana being Sunday. The girl smiled sweetly at me and replied, *"Yes, nine till one"*.

Having detected the smell of steaks grilling on charcoal, the skipper led the stampede into a beautiful open-air restaurant set amid jacaranda trees. My fish soup was exquisite, closely followed by fillet steak and chips, then fresh mangoes and ice cream, which may have been the best in the world. A few glasses of *'vino collapso'*, then back to the boat which rolled enthusiastically in a cross swell all night. I vowed to put out a stern anchor in the morning to keep her nose to the seas. Pitching is tolerable but rolling is vile.

Next morning, Else, who was purser as well as first mate and medical officer, went through the accounts of the voyage sorting out IOU's and various petty transactions.

Later we went for a long walk up the steep valley side and marvelled at the strange crops and mode of cultivation on the terraces. Cows were kept individually in attractive little thatched houses. None seemed to be free to graze but all looked well and content. We dined that night at the same restaurant, where I tried scabbard fish, which is a long, and ugly eel like fish caught in immense depths round the island of Madeira. My reasoning was that if something is worth fishing for in several miles of water, it must be good. I was not wrong.

Next day, we were off to the boat yard where several large fishing vessels were under construction in timber and all by traditional old fashioned methods including fine use of the adze. It was like stepping back in time. We needed a better piece of timber for our extension bowsprit on which flew our beautiful flying jib. This was chosen, cut, shaped and planed to our direction, all for free by the friendliest folk imaginable. Our interpreter in all this was Michael, a London lad who was repairing and living aboard an old schooner hauled up on the beach. He had picked up a lot of Portuguese and, I thought, may have had an inclination to pick up Vanessa. However, Vanessa was having none of it.

16th September. Off to Funchal, the capital of Madeira, for the mail. This has to be one of the most hair rising bus rides in the world. For much of its route is along a narrow bendy road carved out of a soaring vertical cliff. We had made the mistake, never to be repeated, of sitting on the hindmost offside seat. Every time the bus went round a bend the back end of the bus swung out over five hundred feet of fresh air. The driver hummed merrily as he wrestled with the wheel and I wondered whether he had volunteered for the job or if it had been an alternative to a death sentence. My knuckles were as white as a dog's tooth when we stepped shakily into, and with some surprise, the streets of Funchal.

We eventually found the post office, collected our mail as we were glad to have contact with friends and family left behind, and then strolled round the town whose streets and pavements, like Machico, are paved in exquisite designs of black and white sets. After a coffee here and there and a cake or two, we made our way to the harbour. Funchal is one of the several places in the world where it is traditional for visiting yachts to paint a permanent 'logo' of their vessel on the harbour walls. Some were beautiful works of art and many were very witty.

Back in Machico, we stopped off with Michael for a beer and a *ponche* concocted of limes, syrup and aquadente, very smooth and very heady. Back at the dinghy, we found that Mark had lost an oar, which resulted in one or two cross words. Again, I had more words on the subject of haircuts.

Come back English banks, all is forgiven. Changing money in Spanish and Portuguese banks demands fortitude and preferably a packed lunch. Every thing seems to take forever or maybe we English need to change down a gear or two.

Still it gave Vanessa's clothes a chance to dry, coming ashore in the surf, a large wave sloshed over the stern of the dingy soaking her up to the waist.

For the next few days Else and Sean were quite poorly with sore and swollen throats and tummy upsets. Else went to see a Doctor who was very efficient and prescribed some antibiotics, which soon did the trick. In the meantime the skipper was kept busy making nourishing broths and sending scavenging parties ashore for ice cream. Later, we found an open sewer running into the sea near the anchorage and so putting two and two together, we abandoned our daily swims from the boat and dinghied over to the end of the bay half a mile away. The water here quickly fell away into awesome blue depths from out of which one could easily imagine fearsome creatures emerging. Then we heard that hammerhead sharks had been troublesome lately and that one fisherman had lost an arm whilst trailing his line over the side in this vicinity.

Later in the week, the invalids having turned away from death's door, we all went out with Michael for a meal at a tiny café high up on the hill. After dining variously on chicken, fish and beef, we gravitated back to the boat on a sort of Madeira pub-crawl calling in at various taverns sampling the local 'ponche' and brandies. Some of the bars seemed to be more or less ordinary dwellings but the welcome was always warm and friendly. Michael was teaching us a little Portuguese, the pronunciation of which we found difficult but amusing to the locals.

Next morning, we were off to Funchal with the WK (white knuckle) Bus Company to collect mail from the Post Office and to visit the museum and go wine tasting at the vintners. Robbie Burns was right about the best laid plans for mice and men. The Post Office was closed for half day. The museum was closed for redecorating and the vintners were closed for reasons unknown, so we resorted as usual to eating, drinking and sightseeing. Amongst the sights to be seen was the open-air market where all manner of exotic fruits and strange vegetables were on sale. The air was pregnant with strange smells of sweet, honeyed ripeness and the tang of citrus. We tried the fruit of the prickly pear cactus and voted it OK as a desert lifesaver but not first choice as an after dinner dessert. Close to the market was a café from whence we could hear *fado* music, the haunting, melancholy specialty of Portugal. The vocals and musicianship were brilliant but the subject matter of the songs seemed to be a catalogue of the many ways in which one's love could be unrequited or dashed to pieces by a heartless lover. W. S. Gilbert's *Tit Willow* appeared a cheerful little ditty by comparison. To help dull the pain and offer distraction from suicide we ordered a few bottles of wine and some food, mine being a bowl of crab soup which I thought might not taste too bad if it was diluted a little with salty tears. It was absolutely scrumptious.

The last bus for Machico left at 21.30 and we made it in the nick of time owing to the reluctance of the waiter to make out our bill, a common occurrence we found, despite the most dramatic and eloquent sign language involving tapping of watches, imaginary steering wheels and vroom-vrooms. We all sat on the very back seat of the bus partly, I am sure, as a result of wine induced bravado and euphoria produced by the cessation of the *fado* music. We speculated that the driver must have a beautiful wife or mistress, as he was obviously eager to get home and drove like a fiend. Every time the coach went over a bump, which was often, we five on the back seat were left in a state of levitation. We should have been terrified, if sober.

22nd September. We had arranged for a taxi to show us the sights of Madeira, so all hands were up bright and early though some less bright and some less early than others. We duly met Armando, the taxi man and squeezed ourselves as best we could into the car, the boys taking it in turn to sit by the window. Armando turned out to be a naturalist and a mine of information on things historical and architectural. Madeira is a most intriguing island of contrasts. Steep valleys with terraced sides growing lush and exotic fruits, such as bananas, guavas, mangoes and passion fruits plus vegetables sweeping up to soaring craggy peaks, wild and savage, partly clad with pines and cedars.

Our first port of call was Pico do Ariero, almost 6,000 feet high. The 360-degree view could only be described as stunning and reminded me of photographs of some of the remoter parts of China. Walking in this country would be a breathtaking experience and we resolved to come back and do it. The air was deliciously cool and pine scented. At various heights above sea level the climate embraces the culture of almost every species of fruit, a rare phenomenon indeed, apples, pears, plums, grapes, figs etc down to the lowest levels where semi-tropical species are grown. We were surprised to learn that this jewel of an island was uninhabited until 1419 and that the first babies born there were twins named Adam and Eve!

During our tour, which included some impressive monuments and statues, we saw Our Lady of Peace on

Tierro da Luta dedicated in gratitude for the end of World War I. The massive anchor chains of Allied vessels torpedoed by the Germans in Funchal harbour surround it.

Large areas of willow in the uplands feed a substantial cottage industry of craftwork in this material. As well as all manner of baskets, we saw full sized grizzly bears; lions and even a giraffe, which we thought, would look splendid in the garden at home. Lunch was at an intimate restaurant owned by a friend of Armado. My first course was impressive, if only for its stark frugality, clear water with an egg in it. A small egg had been poached in water to which a drop of olive oil and a bay leaf had been added. And that was it! I afterwards discovered that it's Portuguese name to which I had been attracted meant *poor man's soup*. However, the second course more than made up for the first. Large blades like swords were suspended from a device at the table, on which were skewered tender chunks of beef dripping with garlic butter. The drips were caught on a large chunk of freshly baked crusty bread and were greatly enjoyed by the three of us and Armado. I may say that the dark red wine was liberal. The boys had yet another omelette. It's tough being a vegetarian sometimes.

Off to the mountains again to see 'Curral das Freiras', Nuns Shelter, where one looks down from behind the dubious shelter of a very rustic fence on to an exquisite green valley a dizzying three thousand feet below. Apparently, in the sixteenth century, a band of sisters fled from pirates who had sailed from Africa to loot the rich churches of Madeira. It seems they liked what they found and founded a permanent colony. We were on the way back to Machico after a wonderful day when Armado pointed out an old lady baking bread in a large open wood fired oven by the roadside. I recall that the large flat loaves were called Sunday bread as it was only baked on that day. The smell wafted over to us and I was out of the car in a trice. Money changed hands and two smoking hot loaves were ours for supper with a glass or two of Dao. *"A crust of bread, a flask of wine and thou"*.

23rd September. Preparing to leave Machico for Funchal. Water in the oil again.

Using the oil changing hand pump, I pumped out the water until the pump started sucking oil. We hauled anchor at about 15.00 and dropped it again outside the marina off Funchal about 18.30.

Else and I fancied a meal ashore by ourselves, so on with the glad rags and into the dinghy. After a stroll up and down the waterfront to see what was on offer, we settled down to a cosy little tavern where we were given a glass of chilled Madeira Sercial as an aperitif. Sercial is the driest of the four Madeira wines, fortified and like a fino sherry. Next in order is Verdelho, a subtle flavoured amber wine, and then comes Boal, a fragrant semi sweet desert wine, then sweetest of all the well known Malmsey which is a no-nonsense dessert wine honeyed and mellow. This wine apparently enjoys travel and several months in a sailing ship present no problem. We bought several bottles which managed to travel unopened to England! A fact, which was later, entered into the log! Anyway, back to the meal. Some deliberation, which is always a good first course, was followed be a most splendid sea food platter for two with crab, mussels, octopus, prawns, shrimps, langoustine and tuna on a huge bed of salad. I seem to remember more than one bottle of vinho verde helping it down.

Next day we dinghied into town – 200 yards – after watching two snorkellers diving for octopus by our vessel. Checking with customs is always a necessary chore at every port of call. As a rule the Portuguese are very bureaucratic but nice with it whereas others are equally bureaucratic with a generous helping of irritability. One just has to bite the bullet. We bumped into Barry and Gill from *Agincourt* who anchored close to us in Machico.

Barry mentioned that he too had suffered an attack of *Montezuma's revenge* in Machico but was now on the mend. They had voyaged from the Azores islands where they had been for two months and about which they were wildly enthusiastic. We determined to call there on the way back. Barry and Gill were on an extended world 'walkabout', working when the money ran short and living off the land or the sea as much as possible. Gill's elderly mother May, a game old girl in her mid-seventies, would fly out regularly to join them for a few weeks wherever their travels took them. We did not know it then but we were to bump into this very jolly pair for the next 6,000 miles. Ocean voyaging is like that. You will be sitting on deck or in some waterfront bar sipping an iced rum and lime when a dot on the horizon resolves itself into familiar masts and sails last seen maybe three thousand miles and an ocean away. You screw up your eyes to make sure, and the excitement mounts. Old sea dog expressions fly thick and fast in heavy Robert Newtonish accents. *"Bring us me spy glass, it's Agincourt on the larboard bow, as I live and breathe. I know 'er by the cut of 'er mizzen"*.

The harness cask. When we were in Machico Bay, Gill and Barry came over to *Ospray* for a drink. After a while Gill asked what we kept in the cask in the galley. Now, in the old sailing ships all of the ship's meat was kept in what was known as the harness cask. Whether this was a reflection on the flavour of the meat I do not know but, thinking to be absurdly nautical and as a blow for independence, we had secured a cask, albeit a plastic one, and made up a brine solution which, according to a recipe in an old book should be 'strong enough to float a potato'. In it we had packed beef, pork, lamb, pheasants and a couple of rabbits. My pride knew no bounds. *"Oh that"*, I said airily, *"that is our harness cask"*. I could see at once that they were impressed. *"Really?"* said Barry and asked what we had salted away. *"I'll show you"*, I said generously and began to ease off the tight fitting lid. There was a faint but sinister hiss like the first warning from a cobra. Then the most appalling stench which cleared the cabin like a charge of grape shot. Within seconds Barry and Gill with May were in their dinghy rowing away lustily. *"You'll have to give us the recipe"*, shouted Barry, with tears rolling down his cheek.

Else and Ness were dispatched to locate and bring back a load of ice, about 80 pounds in fact. A golden rule, especially in Latin countries, is always send the girls to negotiate with the fellows. An hour or so later, sure enough, back they came. Else at the oars and Ness sitting atop one of the three large sacks of ice. She swore it would ruin her love life for years to come. Meanwhile, the boys had gone off to paint our logo on the sea wall amongst others. Off we went to inspect. They had done a brilliant job depicting *Ospray* sailing off into the sunset.

Later we went on to the supermarket for a big shop as we depart for the Canaries tomorrow but only three days distant so we are fairly relaxed. We sat up late on deck under a full moon chatting and sipping a glass or two of wine.

25th September. After a quick nip into town for petrol and paraffin for the generator and lamps, we hauled anchor at 11.50 and under a light breeze filling the Genoa, we slipped down the coast to Camara de Lobos (the lair of the sea wolves) where the early settlers had found a colony of seals. The village is very much a working fishing harbour. Beautifully kept fishing boats all painted in bright colours came to roost every evening with their days catch. The waters round Madeira are rich in fish and huge marlin, swordfish and tuna feature with the humble but tasty sardine. The sea cliffs here are reputedly the second highest in the world, rearing up to almost two thousand feet.

By early afternoon, we headed the bowsprit seawards, hauled up the main and shaped our course for Lanzarote, the easternmost island in the Canaries. I was feeling just a bit queasy; a common symptom first day out not helped by a fluky wind, constantly changing in direction and strength, the usual effect in the lee of a high island. This demanded constant attention to the sails which filled and emptied, dropping their blocks on the deck with a wallop then snatching them peevishly up again.

The preventer guy leading from the end of the boom to a strong point aft (to prevent a gybe) would fall slack when the huge mainsail dropped the fetch up with a sickening jolt when it filled again. No- one got much sleep that night.

However, by dawn we were emerging from the wind shadow of Madeira and a beautiful sunrise greeted us as if to say sorry for a lousy night.

With two reefs in the main we sailed into a sun drenched day with a lusty north-easter bowling us along at six knots. I have conjunctivitis and a tummy upset, possibly from Machico.

A large school of dolphins – over a hundred – joined the ship for an hour or so, romping towards us with their usual infectious glee. We hung over the rail watching their antics as they took turns riding our bow wave and looking up at us with their merry little eyes. The boys tried to touch them with bare feet by hanging from the bowsprit but they would not allow that. Nearly, but not quite. Never in all my life, have I seen such jolly creatures as dolphins and it was re-assuring to see big packs roaming the oceans. They seem to love the company of humans and boats and when we were down below decks we could often hear their squeaks as they chattered to each other – or to us – who knows? After a while they left us to seek other diversions and half an hour later we saw them romping over the horizon like a bunch of kids let out of school.

That night, the water was glowing with phosphorescence and Else said that when the full moon rose, the fingers of spray flung by *Ospray's* bows as she plunged through the night, were like handfuls of emerald necklaces.

Chapter 3

The Dramatic Canary Islands

Land was sighted on the bow about 17.00 hours on the 27th September. About 20.30 hours, we identified the flashing beacon on Punta Pechiguera. One long flash of eleven seconds and three short ones every fifteen seconds. We also speculated on the sources of other lights we could now see. One long row was attributed to the camel stables of the foreign legion's outpost on Lanzarote! We were slightly apprehensive about coming into an unknown harbour in the dark especially when Else did a plot which put us firmly on dry land! The sounds coming from beneath the boat were still very liquid ones but nevertheless we headed out a little and away from the flash of breakers, which we could see when, the moon came out from behind a cloud.

"Beyond the surf, beyond the waves that roar,
There may indeed – or may not – be a shore".

Two miles further and we identified the red light at the end of the breakwater. We crept round and after sniffing round the harbour in the dark, we found two yachts at anchor so we decided to jump into bed with them, so to speak, and accordingly rounded up and dropped the anchor. A gentle burst astern on the engine and *Ospray* gave her usual little quiver, which told us all was fast on the bottom. It was 04.15 hours. From the shore the first sounds we heard was the ra ra, ra ra ra of a bunch of lager louts, no doubt British, returning to their digs from a night out. Several thoughts crossed my mind, the most charitable of which involved machine guns. However, *"sleep that knits the ravelled sleave of care"* soon put me away with the best of them.

When we awoke to brilliant sunshine, we found that our port side neighbour was *Agincourt*.

First impressions of our surroundings failed to ignite much enthusiasm. A monumental volcanic eruption lasting for several years occurred in the 1700's and covered the island in cinders. Lots of new development, some of it slightly garish conveyed an image of a gigantic slagheap with a slice of Blackpool tacked on to it. On going ashore, dozens of car rental shops vied with cafés desperately trying to make us Brits feel at home with offers of 'Full English Breakfast', 'Roast Beef and Yorkshire Pud', 'Fish and Chips' or for the more adventurous 'Roast Chicken' with chips of course, all preceded, accompanied or followed and frequently all three, by lashings of beer.

The cactus growing on the front gardens must seem quite an intrusion on the Englishness of it all and no doubt some entrepreneur will import plastic dahlias before long to replace the alien blemish. Our cynicism took a step backwards when we discovered there were no donkey rides to be had on the beach but one could hire a camel, though we did speculate that these may have been the not so good looking ones rejected from the foreign legion. Matters improved even further next day when we hired a car and toured the island. Our first stop was Teguise where an open air market had a distinctly Moroccan feel; as well it might, being quite close. We were vastly impressed by the stallholders, many of whom were multilingual and could converse freely in six or eight languages. This made me, at least, reappraise our values in education.

High quality leather goods predominated but at the other end of the scale were quite attractive sandals, cunningly contrived from car tyres, also beautifully painted farmyard animals cut from beaten oil drums for use as trays, fire screens etc. Reluctantly we left this oasis and hit the road to visit the castle of Santa Barbara. By this time the sky had become dark and rain driven by a near gale was lashing the castle – it rarely rains in Lanzarote – which was perched as it was on a hill of cinders surrounded by miles of desolate lava strewn moonscape came quite low on my list of des. Res's. We had taken a picture showing Else, Vanessa and Sean huddled in their jackets and leaning at 45-degree angle trying to descend the castle stairs against the fury of the wind.

We saw no visible water on Lanzarote though it is in man's nature to strive to grow plants. Wine is produced here and each vine crouches miserably in the shelter of a little semi-circular wall built of lava against the drying trade winds. After a tour round the Cuevos de los Verdes, enormous caverns inhabited in times long past by a people called the guanches; we went for a bread and cheese lunch on a beach of black volcanic dust and lava. No signs of life were to be seen. No birds. No seaweed. So seeking, like Mr and Mrs Ramsbottom, for further amusement we set off in search of camel trekking but lost our way and ended up in the *Montanas del Fuego*. The mountains of fire were well named and the impression was of a fire of unbelievable magnitude only just extinguished. Weird is too faint a word to describe a landscape piled high in a jagged chaos of destruction with house sized cinders vomited from the earth in terrifying peristaltic convulsions. The only sign of life was a trace of sulphur yellow lichen. No plant had colonized this hostile area in over two hundred years.

We were glad to leave the Devil's Kitchen as darkness was falling and only the tops of Los Montanas Fuegos were glowing red in the last rays of the setting sun and shining through the eye holes of the iron devils lurking by the roadside.

By the time we reached the harbour, we were all famished, so we slipped into a restaurant, which turned out to be a bit more upmarket than we realised. A day spent clambering round volcanoes leaves one a touch short on sartorial elegance but we stuck it out and dined quite grandly on sirloin steak and Roquefort cheese. Two bottles of lusty red wine and we were rowing back to *el barco negro* (as the Spaniards called her) where we spent a rolly night.

Two days later and we were up early to depart Lanzarote for Fuertaventura, the next Canary to the west as it were.

Our normal procedure was to hoist the dinghy on to its davits on the stern before every trip. However, a calm sunny day, short 50 mile hop and bone idleness conspired to make me decide to tow it behind us. Bad decision. Out of the lee of the land the seas became boisterous and a strong current threatened to sweep us in to the slavering jaws of a reef reaching hungrily out from Isla de Lobos (Wolf Island). As we ran down the coast to Rosario, the sea became quite hearty and the dinghy was fetching up with a horrid jolt on its painter despite me rigging a shock absorber. Within one mile of Rosario, the painter snapped leaving the dinghy adrift in a strong breeze. I started the engine and clapped her hard astern to allow Mark to board the dinghy forgetting about the broken rope which instantly went round the prop stopping the engine. Now we were in a pickle. No engine and the dinghy away like a lamplighter. Mark very bravely stripped his trousers and leapt over the side with Else holding a rope attached to his waist. Alas the rope came to a stop before the lad had reached the dinghy and after playing him like a salmon for a few seconds, Else released him and he shot forward. A few seconds later we saw, across the billows, Mark's bare behind flop over the dinghy's side. A cheer went up from all hands on *Ospray*.

Mark's brief was to motor into Rosario to summon help, if we should need it, while we would try to sail into harbour in the gathering darkness. The leading lights into the harbour were very difficult to discern and we found ourselves in the grip of a south leaving current that threatened to sweep us past Rosario and down the coast. However, by pinching the wind as much as possible we just made it to the entrance where we met Mark just as we lost the breeze. Mark caught our thrown line and took us in tow, at a snail's pace to be sure, but heading to the inner harbour half a mile away.

We had not gone far when a pilot boat came out and throbbed to a halt alongside us and took over the tow rope. I had been warned to beware of salvage claims in these kinds of circumstances and to always negotiate a fee, so

I was a little worried. After reading of some unfortunate experiences reported in the yachting press, we had been worried about a hefty claim for salvage whereby a vessel which 'rescues' another vessel may claim part of the ship's value according to the degree of danger she was in. *Ospray* was in no real danger but sometimes these things are interpreted very liberally. Needlessly, as it happened, for Juan the pilot was generosity itself. After helping tuck *Ospray* into a snug berth he disappeared refusing to entertain any reward saying with an eloquent shrug, *"I help you, maybe one day you help me"*.

When Juan had gone, we learned more of Mark's exploits foraging for help on shore. As previously mentioned he was trouserless and clad only in a wet, stretched jersey, which barely covered his credentials even when held down. Trying to explain the plight of *Ospray, el barco negro* and the requirements for her help to foreigners needed the use of sign language and gesticulation. He said it was only the change of expression on the ladies' faces, which reminded him of other considerations.

A fiesta was in full swing in Rosario with many stalls selling food and drink whilst belting out music at top whack. Many of the stalls smoke and savoury smells swirling from charcoal grills, advertised *carne de cabra*. Now I have never eaten goat meat and taking a strong fancy to it set off finding the best bargain. Not a morsel was to be found. Apparently the wily old *cabras*, working on the principle of letting other's shipwrecks be your landmarks, on the first sign of a fiesta had hightailed it for the mountains. Whilst Else and Vanessa were pining for fresh meat, particularly for me *carne de cabra,* the boys required vegetarian fare and we traipsed for miles without success. The Canarians seemed not to understand the meaning of the term. At last we found a café that had a large pot full of soup which appeared to be thick with vegetables. We sank down and ordered cold beers while our soup was dispensed. Mine had a large gobbet of meat from unknown and mysterious origins. I hid it behind my vegetables and spent the next twenty minutes devising cunning ways of distracting the lads' attention whilst I hacked a piece of meat off with my spoon and devoured it. So I went *cabraless* to bed.

Early next morning, a smart car drew up by us on the harbour wall and two smartly uniformed officials jumped out and greeted Else and me with broad smiles, which was an improvement on past experiences. *"Buenos dias senor y senora. You come plis"*. The car door was held open for us and we were whisked away to customs and immigration to fill in numerous forms, all in quadruplicate without carbon paper.

Juan came round later and took us several trips into town for gas oil (eight five gallon drums), sixty pounds of ice and a pile of groceries, then for a ride to the airport seeking a flight for Vanessa to return home.

This Canarian gent took us well and truly under his wing and called almost every day. All of this between his duties as the port pilot. We went off to see an immense but beautiful – it is really me saying this – new holiday development populated entirely by Germans. Everything laid on for a happy holiday. Bingo, tombola, shops, crèches, restaurants and of course swimming pools where I speculated as to whom complained about whom grabbing the best beach chairs! He took us for a drive round the northern part of the island, which was like a chunk of the Sahara with a strange desolate beauty. Among the wind-sculptured hills of sand a sibilant whisper told stories of millenniums ago. We drove back through the interior, which is starkly barren except for the odd palm tree and prickly pear. I can't for the life of me imagine how anyone scratches a living, apart from tourism to which the island contributes only sand and sun but an abundance of both.

I was forced to confront Juan with the legend that Fuertaventura was once lush and green until the Spanish came with their goats and hunger for timber. Juan gestured expressively *"Sempre seco"* he said. Always dry. This may have been loyalty to his Spanish forbears though it is said that Canarians dislike being called Spanish.

Juan was as keen to practise his English as we were to exercise our meagre Spanish. He certainly had the edge but we got along famously, Juan having a quick grasp of even quite subtle jokes and leg pulls. "*Muy seco*", with a finger drawn across the throat was the signal for the tattered old car to be swung in a cloud of dust onto the yard of a lonely taverna for a cold beer.

3rd October. Departed Rosario with warm memories and a pilot book for the Canaries (in Spanish), 'Costa Occidental de Africa' with a card inside. "*To my friends, it is nice to meet a united family*".

With a brisk wind from astern, staysail and jib boomed out goosewinged either side of the ship, we sped down the coast gazing at the austere beauty of the mountains forming the spine of the island until just before 6pm when we rounded the harbour wall and tied up in Moro Hable on the southern tip of Fuertaventura. We passed on the sea a nudist beach on which also lay the wreck of a schooner half buried in the sand. The schooner was studied for some time through our strongest binoculars. As is the custom in the harbours the world over our ropes were caught and cleated by anyone standing around which in this case was the young and handsome harbour master and Dutchman Jan, who dwelt on an old vessel, moored bow and stern next to *Ospray*.

The harbour wall would have won an award by the ships repairers' guild having a bulge contrived to catch and rip off a vessel's rail on the rising tide. However, we rigged up a plank fend off which merely required someone to get up and move it several times during the night. It also formed a convenient bridge for cockroaches to board us simply by walking rather than by flying aboard. So when I got up barefoot in the night, I trod with some care thinking to save myself the trouble of climbing back down the mast. The very first night, I perceived in the dim light of the moon, a large specimen marching resolutely over the bridge clicking like a clockwork mouse. I seized the boathook and turfed it into the sea. I hope cockroaches don't swim but I suspect they do. The most successful creature ever is not going to have such a flaw. Quite often, if you accidentally step on a cockroach, there will be a sickening crunch, and then the creature will gather together all the bits and reassemble them before marching off slightly miffed by the inconvenience. It is said that if cockroaches infest a boat they will crawl onto a sleeping person to lick the moisture from around the eyes and mouth. Well, all I can say is, if I wake up to such an occurrence, I hope *el cucaracha* is wearing earplugs!

I soon decided that we should have a walk up the beach to view the wrecked schooner. What an eye opener? No wonder the lads had disappeared each day. The further up the beach, the fewer clothes were in evidence until long before we reached the schooner all was laid bare. Mostly German, they came in all shapes and sizes through S and M to XL, XXL and upwards bestrewn on the beach like elephant seals and the sea waiting patiently to come in. Some played volleyball or frolic ball in the surf happily oblivious to the effects of gravity or kinetics. Vanessa was disgusted and Else was intrigued but refused to join me in a skinny dip, so I abandoned the idea, thereby denying the world a glimpse of my naked body.

Later that evening after a meal and a glass or two of wine in a café, I phoned my brother Mike and he told me gently that my old dog Misty had died. My chary entry reflects my mood at the time.

6th October. "I feel racked with remorse and feel that I have betrayed her by coming away knowing full well she would have never left me in the same way. I think she gave up the will to live when I was no longer with her. Goodbye little friend. Had to go for a long walk to let go my feelings".

7th October. Hand still very painful from a tendon injury sustained when I grabbed a flogging sheet a couple of weeks ago. Decided I should go up to the mast head to turn the masthead light as I had stupidly faced it the wrong way when re-stepping the mast showing starboard as port and vice-versa. We have been sailing at night with paraffin running lights since then.

I would normally climb the ratlines and slip with the bosun's chair which was attached to the jib halyard and then be winched the rest of the way on the anchor gypsy. Now climbing the mast is another job for which one is unlikely to be killed in the rush. Even in the calm conditions prevailing it was attended with slight apprehension which went up a few notches when as I neared the top I could see that the shackle pin on which I was suspended had worked loose and was about to fall out, hanging, as it transpired, by a single thread. The mousing on the shackle had either come adrift or been omitted!

We were up early to clear for Gran Canaria, heading for an anchorage near to Gando on the east coast. The wind was blowing very fresh with a lumpy sea until we cleared the acceleration zone some miles offshore. With things more settled we put out a trolling line and soon hooked and lost a decent fish but almost immediately hooked and landed, after a tussle, an 8lb skipjack tuna. When I tapped it on the head for supper Mark stalked below in a huff.

We arrived in the bay near Gando under lowering skies. Whilst preparing to anchor, a large inflatable was launched from the shore by a gang of soldiers who appeared to be squabbling with each other and bungling the whole procedure. After sorting out who was doing what, they made towards us and began swearing invective at us and making threatening gestures with their automatic rifles. I picked out a few recognizable words from their tirade, the kindest of which was "Vamoose". So, being unsure of our welcome that is what we did.

After dawdling about in the next bay for a while we decided that the pros of having an easy meal with a bottle or two of wine did not compete with the cons of a possible military mid-night boarding party, so yet again we 'vamoosed' shaping our course for Arginegen on the southern tip of the island. We passed Mas Palomas, the cape of many pigeons at about 21.00 and after some searching we picked out the feeble port and starboard entrance lights of Arginegen harbour and cast anchor about 22.30. Else had cooked a tasty broth totally forgetting about my prize tuna. However, I recovered from this affront, ate greedily of the soup, drank deeply of the good red wine and fell fast asleep.

8th *October.* Awoke to find ourselves in a mini ghetto of English boats amongst whom was Pete, a single hander, who professed to be unsociable but could talk for England storing up all his lonely thoughts at sea and downloading them when amongst people again. I think we were the first he had met since leaving England.

Pete gave us some instruction in astro-navigation on which he was something of a pundit. Astro-navigation is not easy despite calculators and allegedly short cut methods, you still have to stand on a reeling deck clutching a sextant and in the short time at dusk and dawn when both the stars and the horizon are visible, then having identified certain key stars, often quite faint in the heavens, measure the angle of a star from the horizon with great accuracy on the sextant. All this while clinging to whatever support you can grab.

Then a full page of calculations using sight reduction tables is required. I doff my cap to the sailors of old who accomplished this with only the most meagre of education. Whilst Sean was our wizard of the wireless, Mark was the brightest star in our little firmament on Astronav. He fell briefly from grace when he lost my watch over the side and came in for some ribbing when he emerged, like Dracula, into the dusk one evening declaring his intention to find Aldebaron. Sean said he had always thought that Hilda Baron was the barmaid at the 'Rose and Crown'.

However Pete's ace in the hole, especially with the lads, was his artistry with the banjo. Else cooked a fine meal and we had a whale of a jam session with Mark on guitar and voice and a little twiddle, now and again, on melodeon by JFM.

Next morning we found a café where one could and did have an English breakfast for £1.20. *Ospray's* crew very nearly increased by one at this juncture. Several families of feral cats dwelt in the rocks which formed the breakwater and we considered kidnapping a kitten for a ship's cat. We had no rats or mice aboard so there would be no work for puss as chief rodent officer. The other function often fulfilled by dogs and cats is as a go between when hostilities exist twixt husband and wife or other family members when direct communication seems undesirable – "Puss, tell your mother she is a miserable, sharp tongued old besom and I will have another beer if I fancy one!" However as we were basically a happy crew with only the occasional growl, the idea was dropped.

Vanessa had decided to fly home as although she fitted in well and enjoyed our times in port she could not face a long ocean voyage across the Atlantic with the prospect of lumpy seas and permanent seasickness. On the eve of her departure we took her out for a farewell dinner at a waterfront café, which won our custom by displaying banana splits on the menu.

9th *October*. The alarm was set for 5am. Ness was up before us, very nervous and taut as a violin string at the thought of travelling alone and changing planes despite our somewhat tongue in cheek assurances that nothing could go wrong. I expect she will miss us, as we will her. After all you can't have <u>two</u> musketeers! After 'posting' Ness through the correct aperture at the airport, it was with a little sadness that we found an English breakfast and I found an English newspaper with an English crossword. It's grand to travel and see the world. This seafaring is all very well but a touch of civilization now and again works wonders. During a wander around Santa Cruz we sat down on a park bench under a huge rubber tree which oozed latex and caused me to dream up a brilliant article for a gardening magazine. 'Grow your own Wellies'.

The long bus ride back to Aguinegin was dreary, dry and dusty, through country resembling a building site. Back on board, the boat had been tidied and a stiff wind was blowing causing us to put out a second anchor, our 60 pounder, the main anchor being 75 pounds. We still dragged a little in the night and next morning all but two vessels, out of twelve, had departed for more shelter. One had snapped his cable losing an anchor.

As the wind was settling a little we decided to go up into the mountains so a car was hired. First port of call was the 'Disa' station to fill our gas bottles. Security was high priority and the clerk at the gate obviously took his duties very seriously for on his right side dangled a six-shooter whilst on his left side, possibly to cope with a misfire or administer a coup de grace, was a long and sinister truncheon. However, we soon had our bottles filled for a third of UK price and departed unscathed to see the mountains.

Much of the lowland is raw and unattractive but as soon as you climb into the region of grass and pines, the scenery improves with every yard. The mountains of Gran Canaria are breathtaking in their grandeur and soon we were amongst pine trees, grass and ferns. We stopped to smell the pines and listen to the birdsong, then found a grove of wild almonds, which were intensely almondy, so we picked some for a Christmas cake.

Later, on the way down at about 4000 ft, we discovered lots of wild figs which were delectably sweet. We were hurrying by now, down the crazy mountain roads zigzagging along horrendous precipices. We were intent on visiting Sioux City for a Wild West evening the highlight of which for me was a performance of the can-can. The scene was set, long before we reached Sioux City, when we passed through a region for all the world like Arizona with huge buttes standing sentinel in the cactus covered badlands. However, when we arrived the show was nearly over. So with regrets for the can-can and barbecued T-bone steaks, we went off seeking for further amusement which we found at a bar in Las Palomas, in the shape of a trio of singing Canarians – no not canaries. Four happy hours later, we tumbled out replete with vino and a hearty supper and beautiful melodies with guitar and mandolin ringing in our ears. Else had elected to drive which was just as well. Vanessa said that she didn't mind missing Sioux City as she thought that the can-can and too much red meat was a dangerous combination leading me to run amok!

12th *October*. Loaded up with 15000 pesetas worth of food and drink from the *Mercado*, as usual discarding all cardboard boxes for fear of importing cockroaches.

Peter came on board, so as a mechanic, I picked his brains about our generator which had begun to smoke badly when running. Pete's diagnosis was instant. Plastic as plastic is an insulator, charred plastic as carbon is a conductor. Discard charred plug. End of problem. "Cheers Pete!"

Next morning in clearing weather we dived to untangle our twisted anchor cables. Mount Teidi on Tenerife could be seen soaring above the clouds 60 miles away giving us something to aim at on the next leg.

14th *October*. After getting the ship ready for off on the morrow all hands slipped away for a couple of beers at a German bar in town. The barman was a caricature of a Bavarian with a huge and splendid moustache and belly to match. Rousing marches were played non-stop on the tape deck amid cries of 'javol'.

It was sometime later and thankfully quite dark when with the music ringing in our ears we tumbled out of the bar and marched back to the boat getting our thigh slaps mixed up with our goose steps with the very occasional 'Heil Hitler'.

Next morning up while still dark, tea and toast, then up with the anchor and away past Peter standing in his hatchway to wave goodbye. In the acceleration zone the wind picked up to about force six with a peevish head sea which slammed against the hull causing torrents of spray over the whole ship and whacking the mainsheet block on the aft cabin roof bringing many a doze to a premature halt. These bangs sound much louder inside the ship than on deck and the skipper's alarmed and indignant face in the hatchway was greeted with puzzled frowns by the boys on duty.

Under a press of canvas we were soon flying past the huge red rock of the Costa del Silencio, where it is said that the pop music from shore side Discos is quite deafening! After rounding the south western tip of Teneriffe we ran into quieter waters and were soon in the bay of Los Christianos which was crowded with other yachts at anchor. After padding around for a little while we found a niche as we thought and were just about to drop the hook when we were startled by a bad tempered and raucous query from a Kiwi skipper if we were not too close? This was the biggest space available and we were confident about our big anchor holding fast in the conditions forecast so we stayed put and wished our friend a pleasant stay in the northern hemisphere. We thought he must have had a bad hair day, as the Kiwi crews we met were always easy going and friendly.

Los Christianos until a few years ago was a peaceful fishing village. It is now a concrete jungle with wall-to-wall cafes and bars offering much the same menus for much the same prices. To break the monotony here and there was a newsagent stacked high with girlie magazines in all languages while a stone's throw away with only the meagrest of covering, basking and frolicking on the beach was the real thing in the flesh.

Close by *Ospray*, lying peacefully at anchor sleeping with head under wing was *Sara* with John and Andy last seen in Machico. They had been caught up in the time- share game and told us all about it. This is a game of bluff on both sides. Touts are sent out, paid per enquiry, to cajole, persuade and bribe couples twixt 25 and 65 to visit time share properties with a view to purchase a transaction involving lots of money albeit for some very plushy apartments, some with swimming pools and no end of tempting features. The tout's job is to get you signed up for a visit and the bait for this may be three days of free car hire or two bottles of spirits or 200 cigarettes. Sometimes money is offered, maybe 5,000 pesetas and a free taxi to the apartment block.

Then it all starts to get a bit shady; the touts enter into a conspiracy with the 'punters' about what to say and what not to say. Couples must be married. They must <u>not</u> live on a boat or be a backpacker and for some reason must not take more than seven weeks holiday per year.

Primed with this information it is not unknown for the occasional long-term ocean wanderer to circumvent rules. We even heard of two ragged sailors who tossed up as to which would turn up in drag as the other's wife. The loser was under strict orders to keep his mouth shut and his hands, which were like shovels, out of sight. We were treated to a demonstration of his coquettish glances and other devices, which he practised before the visit. I thought my pants would never dry, as they say. Back to the visit. On arrival one is greeted with a drink then shown around the condominium and one or two typical apartments, some of which are quite stunning. Then comes the pressure. Back to the reception lounge, each couple to separate table and salesman who, whilst very matey and jolly, carefully steers the questions and manoeuvres one into a corner. You admit that you like the set up and yes you would love to spend a few weeks a year in such a place or swap it for somewhere equally grand in the Seychelles or other exotic location. Wouldn't it be nice to take and impress your friends? Yuck!

You are meant to feel obligated for wasting so much of the nice salesman's time. If you do not give a positive *No*, the salesman will bring his boss over who will usually come up with an extra special unmissable, today only offer. He pushes this with intimidating vigour. Should you fail to grasp this generous offer ignoring all his hard work and self-sacrifice, he will insult your decisiveness and your sanity, and then stalk off in a huff to find game that will stand still and be shot at. Every so often a bell will ring, a champagne cork will pop and an announcement made to the crowded room that Mr and Mrs Joe Bloggs have taken up weeks 39 and 51 for apartment 1729. The whole ordeal is so unpleasant and manipulative that we know of several who were stung into retaliation, milked the system and sailed away laden to their marks with booze and fags.

Mark and Sean were taken by the idea of going as a couple but could not settle on who should Be Mister and who Missus. Else and I considered Sean the logical candidate for Missus with his sparkling smile and curly hair. We decided that for one of Else's dressed to look right on his tall boyish figure, there would need to be supplements added in certain areas. This was no problem except that no one could stop laughing long enough to make sensible suggestions and we took seriously the danger of Sean being picked up or even indecently assaulted on his way back to the vessel.

A car we hired for the three days on the first of which we drove up Mount Teidi. An astonishing journey up, up, up and up through baron landscapes with only lava and prickly pears, which gradually merged into figs and almonds the fragrant pine forests.

Suddenly on rounding a sharp bend there was Teidi looming high above everything. All around were great crags and peaks in the weirdest shapes and colours from red through ochre and yellow to umber in the shadows rearing from the mountain desert land in the clear sweet air. Quite breathtaking!

A cable car takes one up another thousand feet, then a stiff climb on foot to the summit where a spectacular view over nearly all of the Canaries of at least fifty miles radius. The tops of the other islands appear to be floating in a white sea.

All around the summit wee fissures in the rocks exuding acrid sulphurous fumes betraying the origins of the mountain as volcanic. Descending to the high plateau we lingered for five hours painting and taking pictures, mesmerised by the lost world weirdness of the peaks rearing around us. One Million Years B.C. and Planet of the Apes were filmed here and one could easily imagine Godzilla silhouetted behind a lofty pinnacle. A distressed Ursula Andress may have won the vote if choice were given.

Nose contest in the Canaries!

Jim on Mount Teidi.

Else on Mount Teidi.

As the sun sank behind the jagged skyline, giant shadows leapt across our view. When the Lord gave out fertile imagination, I suspect I was near the front of the queue, for I quickly decided that I did not want to be here after dark, so suiting actions to thought we whizzed down the mountain at a good speed.

A young German couple came to see us and look over *Ospray*. They took us to see their boat, which was also a steel *Spray* named *Easy*, as they found each of their *Spray* projects easier than the last and not as I would have imagined tedious. *Easy* apparently sailed like a witch being only 12 tons in weight against *Ospray's* 17 tons. This had been achieved by putting in lead ballast low down in the keel and siting all tankage in the keel on top of the lead. Over a ton of fuel could be carried and the same of water. After hull construction all the frames were removed. Hence 12 tons.

14th October. Departed Los Cristianos for San Sebastian on the Island of Gomera about 40 miles away and just visible in a slight haze.

Gomera was the Island that Colombus left from on his voyage of discovery. Whatever the merits of it's geographical location, Gomera had at least one other attraction in the form of one Dona Beatriz der Perona by whom he was entertained? This lady was free at the time having recently murdered her husband during a rendezvous with his mistress, a Guanche princess. Whether this hastened or retarded Christopher's departure for far away places is not known.

We came to San Sebastian at 18.30. The sand on the beach is as black as coal dust and the hillside behind is steep and terraced, speckled with white houses and palm trees. We went ashore for a stroll and a drink, the folk very friendly. No time-shares yet and long may it remain? The village was very pretty and old fashioned. We soon found a snug little restaurant where a flask of red wine was set before us while food was being prepared. Else had pork cutlets which she voted the best ever. I had a fine steak whilst Mark and Sean had pizzas.

The tide had beached the dingy when we returned so a short drag across the black sand as so to bed. All hands quite content! Next morning we were up early to collect the hire car and visit the open-air market for fruit and vegetables for the ocean crossing as our intentions were for a brief stop at Hiero then head for Trinidad.

Lemons at 60p per kg, half a crate of green oranges, half a crate of apples, potatoes, sweet potatoes, green beans, green tomatoes and bananas but no onions. A long voyage without onions is unthinkable and would throw an intolerable strain on the cook's resources.

Then away up into the mountains, the road zigzagging up the steep sides, a wonderful setting for a James Bond car chase. We stopped at a look out and from several thousand feet below us came the faint sound of cocks crowing and dogs barking. On again through crags and pinnacles the dense laurel rain forest, the only one in the world. This dark tangle of jungle is somewhat claustrophobic but within it we found a stream – the first running water in the Canaries. The water tasted a bit jungly as though it may contain water snakes or even alligators but it washed down our lunchtime boccadillos tolerably well. The track eventually emerged from the oppressive laurels onto a precipitous road down the mountain to a valley rich with sweet corn, bananas and all manner of citrus fruits. The heady scent of all this produce filled the air to the drousy hum of insects.

It was Sunday and we took the car back at 09.30 and then spent a lazy day strolling round the town nestling snugly in a cleft in the mountains. We heard a chap conversing from his bedroom window with someone on the far side of the valley about half a mile away by means of the unique whistling language used by the Gomerans. There was speculation about whether the conversation was just idle chatter of major importance such as "Do you fancy a pint and a game of darts tonight?" Mobile 'phones will never catch on here!

By 08.00 next morning, we had the anchor up and were away to Santiago some three hours easy sail. On board we had our German friends Mateus and Ramon. Mateus had married a Spanish girl and in three years has mastered the language. Well I suppose you would, wouldn't you. I recall passing an apartment block in Tenerife. An upstairs window was open. It would seem that some poor hombre had upset his wife and was being given an ear bending. Big time! Like bursts of machinegun fire the tirade continued until we disappeared and probably long after. Maybe it continues still. I have often wondered what the fellow had done but even for genocide the price seemed high.

Under staysail we lazed along at about three knots. I put a line out baited with a sardine and almost immediately had a strike, after a short but brisk battle, Else netted a bonito of about 5lbs. The bait had hardly re-entered the water when it was taken by another, the twin of the first. This was our ration, one for us and one for our friends, so we stowed the rod. The seas in this region must be stuffed with fish.

We nosed into Santiago, which is a cosy little harbour packed with fishing boats but with just enough room alongside the quay for little old us. No sooner were we safely tied up, dues paid and re-iced when the fishing fleet trickled in. Mostly smallish vessels from 18-foot open boats to larger ones of 25 foot with a small cabin and beautiful spoon bows for shedding the Atlantic rollers encountered in these parts. The catch was mainly tuna of 7 to 10 lbs each caught on bamboo poles with live bait from a tank. One boat had well over 200 fish for one days fishing. *Ospray* was greatly admired by the friendly fishermen as a fine fishing boat, which made my day.

I came back on board to find Mark and Sean entertaining a Mr Ballentyne of whisky fame with his lady who had read Slocum's book "Sailing Alone Around the World" and were very interested in our voyage.

Chapter 4

The Smiling Folk of the Cape Verdes

3rd November. Departed Hiero 11.30, indented destination Trinidad approximately three weeks distant. Lots of dolphins, several hundred speckled dolphins, some with babies, outriders guarding the school – big bulls. They stayed with us into the second watch. Our watch system was three hourly, 2pm till 5pm being open, subsequent watches being part of the rota. The 5pm till 8pm watch cooked the evening meal and christened the sundowner, which became a treasured part of the ritual taken at 6pm when the sun was over the yardarm.

Our first day we logged a tolerable 105 miles. The wind for the next few days was light, force 2 to 3 maximum, so under engine. It began to appear that conditions were beginning to favour a destination of the Cape Verdes. This was confirmed later in the day. So this was decided upon.

7th November. Caught two dorado so fresh fish for supper. It was noticed that we were being followed closely by a fish that we named Hungry Horace. Any flying fish that we found on deck in the morning were fed to Horace who we found had a very catholic appetite.

9th November. Gorgeous velvety night. Doing a bit more star spotting. About 20.30 a kestrel came to visit the boat. He hovered around for a while and I awoke Else from a deep and beautiful sleep to see him 100 miles from land! Do kestrels migrate? Or was he taking a holiday? Anyway he slipped sideways like they do and was off. Maybe he was looking for rats on the ratlines! I phoned Dad, bless him, and Sean phoned his Dad. His conversation lasted until Sean mentioned that his Dad was paying for the call.

10th November. Put the rod out and zap came Hungry Horace and seized the bait. Feeling something of a traitor for catching our faithful follower 0f 500 miles, we unhooked him and let him go into his element without delay. He was a fine fellow of about 5lbs.

Shortly after this event we entered the Sound Between Sao Vicente and Santo Atdeo. Visibility was very poor due to the Harmattan and its cargo of Saharan dust. I don't wonder so many ships have been wrecked on the Cape Verdes.

Sao Vicente is a colourful landscape of great crags and red and ochre rocks with vast peaks and pillars. As we sailed into the Bay of Porto Grande a fishing boat was just hauling his nets, a type of purse seine, about ten dark folk were hauling while another kept station with a great oar. We hadn't even got the anchor down before a boat arrived with three local lads offering to look after our boat, and us even offering references. After terminating several quarrels we settled on Alphonso for boatman. A short distance from where we were stationed, an old steamer lies beached, her bones rusting away. While nearby are tethered two old tugs and steamers who belch out great cloud of black smoke. All against a backdrop of a bay surrounded by craggy mountains, one looking like a face in repose – Face Mountain.

We chose Alphonso to look after us during our stay for several reasons. He was a tall statuesque African with the bearing of an African Chief. He took us all over town to buy supplies and everything we bought he arranged a price, which seemed to us to be fair to all concerned. After a few days I was amazed that I trusted him totally. He was beautifully spoken with a quiet dignity. Apparently he had fled Liberia during the troubles there. His father had an important post in the government. One evening came a knock at the door and his father was summoned away. Next morning Alphonso glimpsed a newspaper whose front page held a photograph of a pile of severed heads, one of which he recognised as his father. He raced home, grabbed a few valuables and with his young brother fled to the bush. He eventually made his way to the Cape Verdes.

Alphonso asked us to take him to Britain from where he planned to get to America where he had some contacts. We regrettably refused as the penalty for carrying unauthorised passengers was severe and probably meant forfeiture of the vessel.

I wrote a substantial reference for him which Else typed. We also assured him that if he ever came to England, he could stay with us as long as he liked and I could find him work. The one thing that impresses me most about the Cape Verdeians is the fact that although many of them are dirt poor they smile all day long and it is said that when swimming they often thump a hammerhead shark on the nose to make him go away.

I had made a pact with Mark to have a decent haircut before going to Trinidad. We found a barber's, and Mark agreed on condition that he could also have a Clint Eastwood shave. The rest of the crew sat around watching the event with great hilarity as it soon transpired that the barber was exceedingly short sighted and his shaking hand might indicate Parkinson's. This was a problem with the haircut but when it came to the Clint Eastwood shave this could be hazardous or even life threatening. An unusually tidy looking son was very glad to leave the barber's.

The town of Mindelo is a revelation, very African at first appearance but with lots of Portuguese influence. The streets are thronged with folk selling all manner of produce – some pitiful in quantity and often quality too. A dozen oranges and two or three bunches of shrivelled herbs. The fruit marked is a riot of colour and noise. Bright red pimentos like rubies, masses of green bananas and green oranges and lemons of which we bought a good store. Lots of things we didn't recognise. Everyone beaming away at us offering to try this and that and taking no offence at all when we didn't try. The apples were little bigger than crab apples and of poor taste. Flies were everywhere.

If we thought the fruit market was fly ridden wait till we see the fish market! Wow. All manner of fish laid out with no ice or running water in 80 degrees F. Everything from mighty tuna, of which there seems to be a superabundance from Spain down to here, to sardines. There seemed little evidence of sharp knives in the fish market; the fish was hacked up in quite a rough fashion. Especially tuna, which seems to be part of the staple diet and amazingly cheap. An Irish boat next to us bought one to feed four for 10 escudos or 12 pence.

Some of the local children are beautiful in the extreme with large brown eyes and expressive, intelligent faces. Everywhere, happy smiling faces and laughter – yes what a contrast to the Spanish. I could spend months here and wish we had come here instead of loitering in the concrete jungles of Canaria. This is the real world and no doubt time will catch up here and spoil it for visitors but hopefully improve the lot of the locals a little.

Next day Alphonso took us to Customs and Immigration that lurked behind an unpainted door in a row of unpainted doors on the wharf. Here we were dealt with courteously and even got a stamp on our passports. The Port Authority was equally good and the Port Official, who saw to us – Senor Lopez – though he had a fearsome revolver and a huge truncheon dangling from his belt, was kindness itself and had a twinkle in his eye for the crew of *Ospray*. Soon, for the sum of 55 escudos – about 60 pence – we were both entered and cleared into and from the Cape Verdes.

On the way back, still with faithful Alphonso guiding us we went to look at an old wooden vessel propped up on the beach. A Spray look-alike, if ever there was one. Well there are strong links between the Cape Verdes and Boston so I should love to know the history behind this one. About 48 feet long, built from massive timbers and with the same clipper bow, she had once been a lovely vessel, and even with her old planks gaping from the sun she looked like an old dowager, past her best but with all the dignity in the world. Her old deadeyes were in place and even all the belaying pins. Her anchor and cable were massive. The anchor must have weighed two hundredweight and the stud-linked chain was about ¾ inch.

On the way back to town we passed a 'shop', a tiny stone hovel about 4 feet high and a floor area less than a telephone box. Outside were displayed the wares. A few jars of pickled something or other, sweets, rum or something passing for rum and cigarettes that could be bought singly. Around it squatted the proprietress and her friends and family or maybe they were customers with no money. Mark stopped for a rum but said that whatever it was had a kick like a mule and a similar taste!

There was a group of children that we had become attached to and on our last day we happily parted with sundry items of clothing and food and our spare change. We had enjoyed our visit to the island and with heavy hearts said our goodbyes.

Market Day in Mindelo, Cape Verdes.

Carrying the prize.

Corner shop!

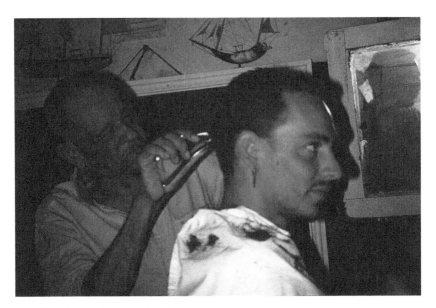

Mark and the short sighted Barber!

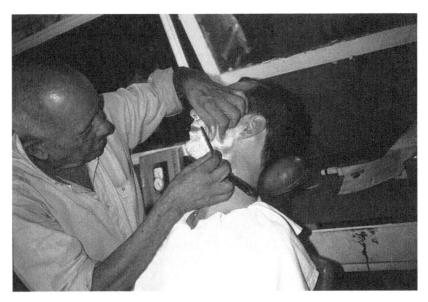

Mark having a 'Clint Eastwood shave'.

Mark on the old Spray.

Sean and porpoise at sea.

Chapter 5

The Lonesome Route Across the Atlantic Ocean to Trinidad

(We had been told that this was a seldom-travelled route – this prophecy came true. In the three-week voyage to Trinidad, we saw not a ship nor a plane nor any other sign of human life. This was such a rarity that it suited us absolutely fine and was nice to know that such situations still existed on this lovely but usually over crowded planet.)

13th November. 14.30 left Sao Vicente with an easterly wind F4 – 5, one reef in the main plus a foresail. As we left the islands and our new friends on the beach, we found strong winds about F7 and boisterous seas until we came out from the wind shadow of the island. Then three days of pleasant sailing knocking off between 100 to 120 miles per day as we gradually settled once more into ocean life. The evening meal became the focal point of the day as we each took turn as cook. Within a few days cocktail hour was established and soon weird concoctions were being presented, not the least successful of which was the 'Ospray Sundowner,' which was presented modestly by the Skipper at the moment when the sun – a blazing crimson ball – just touched the sea as he tucked himself into bed. Although this should be closely guarded secret I will confide it to my diary. A generous tot of brandy, a capful of vino calapso, a snort of lemon and same of lime, a little tonic water topped with a twist of lemon and a large cherry for the sun. Cheers. The evening menu often featured fish, which were normally caught without much trouble and included dorado, bonito, skipjack tuna, all which were powerful fighters, scad and a couple of wahoo, which I believe, are much prized as game fish in the Caribbean and have only recently been found to exist in the Eastern Atlantic. Anyway they take the bait with explosive violence and line screams off the reel at a thumb-scorching rate. Probably the reason for their somewhat avant-guarde name is the sound uttered by the astonished fishermen when one is hooked.

Curries and spaghettis featured often on the menu varying from passable to quite splendid. A litre of wine was always served having set the boat's funds back a mere 40pence. Supper was a jolly time with the lamps burning brightly and everyone in a mood to relax and swap stories. One glass of wine with our meal was never exceeded. Our original rules that "He who cooks does not wash up, has been changed to, he who cooks always washes up", as it was found that some cooks could use an amazing number of pans, pots and utensils, secure in the knowledge that someone else had to clear up afterwards.

The days went by quickly enough. A huge amount of reading was done. Navigation, fiddling with the sails to coax another quarter of a knot from the old girl, repairing damage to sails, an ongoing job. Else is good at this and makes a fine neat job. Preventing chafe is a major problem especially when running down wind with the two genoas set up as twins with booming out poles. There are fore guys, after guys and guys doing jobs you would never imagine, a real cats cradle. Each one doing its best to rub a gap in its nearest neighbour.

Some of the nights are squally and in the darkness a terrifying arch of total blackness comes up astern. The sea assumes a menacing look and the wind suddenly increases to a hooley and rain lashes down in a fury. A couple of days ago our port backstay carried away during one of these and the two forestays went alarmingly slack while the genoa flailed around until we brought her on the other tack and set up the starboard backstay. The frightening thing is the suddenness with which everything happens. Half an hour later the wind is steady again which is more than can be said for the crew's nerves! Last night the watch was beautiful, the last quarter of the moon came out and there was a stiffish breeze from the nor-east and a great majestic sea came rolling up like ranges of hills, some with white frothy tops which you could hear growling and hissing as they approached. Then they would go scrunch under the boat with a smother of foam and go frolicking on their way. An occasional one now and again would throw a bucket full of water into the cockpit just to make sure the helmsman was awake.

A bird flopped into the dinghy in the night and was still there at dawn when I was clinging on to the gallows trying to get a shot of Venus and of the moon. However, I went below to wake Else and when I came back on deck, he had gone. Beautiful sunrise. I had a cup of tea that was foul due to bad water, logical I suppose. So I made another from bottled water. One must have a decent cup of Rosie Lee first thing ack'emma. Baked two loaves, I can smell them now in the oven. Wow,

I shall put the rod out again in a few minutes; last night there was a furious strike, yards of line scorched off then nothing. The trace either snapped or was bitten through. There are flying fish everywhere in great flocks bursting away from the bow. I expect they think *Ospray* is a huge ravenous fish. I don't wonder they scurry. Many of these seas we are looking up at on the approach, sometimes at an appreciable angle. I suggested to Mark that he shinny up the mast with a tape measure and stop when he was level with the tops of the great waves but he displayed no enthusiasm.

The VHF radio which ceased to function a few nights ago has suddenly decided it wants to work for its living again but for how long before it rejoins the dole queue I do not know. Each day we see shearwaters and storm petrels (Mother Carey's chickens). The shearwaters never seem to settle or at least we never saw one on the water but wheel tirelessly skimming the waves. A perfect example of functional design. A thousand miles from land they seem quite at home. I wonder if they sleep on the wing? For 1500 miles we saw no ships or planes and no rubbish or other signs of mankind.

Without these signs of civilization we were blissfully content. The solitude was wonderful if a little awesome. Sometimes the rhythm of the boat as she ploughs purposefully along is wonderfully satisfying, an ancient rhythm as basic as that of lovemaking. At other times, especially with a confused sea, it is widely irritating and evokes explosions of language, even more basic than the rhythms. Such as when I burned my nose on the oven whilst inspecting a cake within.

Henry the Navigator has gone AWOL a couple of times for several days each. The first time being somewhat alarmed, I put a trunk call through to Phillips, who told us that the American army whose satellite we use had taken them out for some reason. Of course we all suspected a war. We then realized that there could indeed be a war and we should not know anything about it for many days or even weeks. What a thought. I wonder what will have changed in the world during our lack of contact? Makes you wonder if it is worth going back with all the wonderful peace out here and the order of things, which has not changed for millions of years. The world could undergo a time warp of thousands of years and we shouldn't even notice.

Quite often, one of the booming out poles would come adrift and have to be lashed into position again. One night after being driven nearly round the bend with the noise of the pole clanging on the deck, I found an old wellie and stuffed the pole into this, then lashed the whole thing in place against the foot of the mast. This worked wonderfully well though a trifle bizarre in appearance, until the pole wore a hole through the toe of the wellie but it still gave us a few nights sleep for which we were grateful.

One institution which became popular especially with Else and I was the bucket shower. A bucket of water was hove from the sea and hung from the end of the boom while one of us stripped and stood under it while the other would tip a great dollop of cool water over him. The first one always evoked a great gasp but after that it was always unbelievably delicious. However the two lads were more circumspect and always sat down to their shower, modesty, well maybe.

About fourteen days out, we contacted Trinidad but the reception was very bad. We were still in good contact with Portishead radio putting through the odd link call the last of which was when we finally sited Tobago on the starboard bow just after midday on the 3rd December, twenty days out from Cape Verdes. Several days before we sighted Tobago, we became aware of a rich composty aroma, that of a tropical island. Trinidad and Tobago ahoy! For this momentous occasion, we had saved a bottle of Champers donated by John Denton, a friend from Shropshire, and with this we toasted our imminent landfall, cheers! After sailing all night we entered the Dragon's mouth off the northern range of Trinidad at dawn with a stiff breeze and all sails drawing well, engine on 2/3 revs. We were making 2.5 knots against a strong tide out of the bocas. As we entered the boca, pelicans and frigate birds soared over us and then to crown it all an osprey swooped down and wheeled over *Ospray* as if in greeting.

> "Oh, the boca at daybreak,
> How can one describe that scene?
> The little emerald islands,
> With the sapphire sea between".

The exotic lushness of Trinidad was in stark contrast to the aridity of the Canaries and Cape Verdes. What a lovely colour is green. Plunging through the furious tide race we eventually popped out into the Gulf of Paria. After a short sail we moored alongside the jetty at Power Boats Ltd. where Else's family were awaiting us. Hugs and kisses and tears of relief from Lill. Eventually the Customs and Immigration arrived; they were there for 07.00 but left and returned. So there we were, eating fresh fruit and drinking coffee or Carib lager sitting on the grass under a palm tree and watching an osprey and a chicken hawk flying overhead with corbeaus in the distance, everyone feeling very satisfied.

We moved the boat up to the Yacht Club and over the next few days visited family and took Mark and Sean sightseeing some of Trinidad's beauty spots and famous beaches. Scarlet ibis, egrets and toucans were some of the birds seen in the mangroves and rain forest. Twelve of us flew to Tobago and hired a maxi taxi for the weekend to experience the wonderful island of Tobago. The small villages with children waving as we drove past, the stunning palm fringed beaches beckoning swimmers into the azure warm waters and the occasional rum punch at the quaint little shops. Tobago is indeed our paradise.

Our stay in Trinidad had been hectic and eventful. We visited Maracas beach, where we always enjoy a shark and bake for lunch and where I lost a tooth while frolicking in the surf. I had four dental appointments with a delightful Trinidadian dentist whose soft and comforting voice was only matched by her soft and comforting bosom, against which she cradled my head whilst working on my jaw. I was in no hurry to leave this chair.

Our hosts have been kindness itself, a car has been provided for our use on many days and the food has been prodigious. I have never seen meat eaten in such quantities and we have been treated to many West Indian dishes of various origins including Creole, which has a delicious and distinctive flavour. Lill's pilau is extremely yummy and once a beef pilau was made for Paul's birthday that would have satisfied the five thousand with a bit left over.

The house at Shirley Bay overlooks the sound between the island of Gasparee on which it is situated at some slight elevation giving a wonderfully commanding view of the shipping coming up and down. Yachts would appear most days coming round the point from first boca or the Dragons Mouth. Each would give rise to speculation as to whether she was one we had met earlier in our travels. The house is a huge open plan tropical house simply built and furnished and without a single pane of glass, all openings being shuttered and louvered. This is where Else learned to swim, fish and sail.

Nelson, the boatman, who looks after the property dwells happily in a small house with his dogs Sputnik and Blackie. A tall lanky Negro with an infectious laugh, Nelson enthralled us with tales of his fishing exploits especially regarding 'de sharks'. He sets pots and traps every day and we calculated he was earning good money at the fish market. So with free house and electricity and many other perks, Nelson has a right to whistle and smile all day.

All too soon, it was time for Mark and Sean to return to Britain, which was experiencing wet and dreary cold weather, -10 degrees. Sean' s father later wrote to me *"Sean had gone away a boy and came back a man"*. He was indeed excellent and useful crew and a pleasure to have on board. Then it was Christmas and arranging for *Ospray* to be hauled out, sandblasted and to have a full paint job with the finest epoxy paint. This was carried out between Christmas and New Year at a very good price. We then moved our gleaming vessel across to Shirley Bay.

Sean, Mark and Jim, just arrived!

Jim with children at Shirley Bay.

Ospray being repainted.

Ospray ready for relaunch.

At anchor in Shirley Bay.

Tobago.

Waterfall in Tobago.

Fun in the water!

Chapter 6

Sails set for the Grenadines and the Windward Islands

Sunday 11th January. Set sail for Grenada after three hours diving to free the anchor rode which had tangled round the ropes to the mooring block and also two of Nelson's grapple multi pronged anchors resulting in the most frightful tangle of ropes and chains. In the end we had to crank up the mooring block on our windlass, as I couldn't get down to it without air tanks. After leaving we were dead into the wind all the way and making dreadfully slow progress under engine only. Slamming into a small but peevish head sea made an uncomfortable passage for our new crew, Else's sister Lill, Paul her brother-in-law and their eight-year-old twins Nicholas and Emily.

During the passage my right eye became very painful and on our first day in St Georges, Grenada I visit a Doctor, who prescribed antibiotics which helped short term. I ended up seeing an eye specialist who said that I had a deep infection and prescribed a variety of drugs that very soon did the trick.

We hired a car and toured Grenada, which is lush and beautiful. All manner of spices are grown and the air is redolent with amazing scent particularly of nutmeg of which I am inordinately fond. The nuts are not picked but gathered when they fall, the yellow husk is removed first leaving the inner husk which is mace leaving the hard familiar kernel of the nutmeg. This is used extensively grated on the local rum punches that vary from island to island and are sometimes quite explosive.

We had tied up in St Georges to a fishing vessel alongside a rickety old wharf, which was infested with cockroaches.

One of my dreads is stepping on a large vigorous roach with bare feet, so my nightly trips to the loo became a nerve tingling adventure. I made a preparation of condensed milk and borax and laid out six place settings throughout the boat in the hope that any visitors would eat heartily.

As on the other islands many of the folk live in shacks varying from extremely rough to very pretty and many of them only eight feet by ten feet or so. The amazing thing is that the numerous children emerge from these tiny dwelling to go to school most beautifully turned out, clean and sparkling with white crisply starched and ironed shirts. The washing equipment usually consists of an old fashioned washboard and indeed we often saw clothes being washed in the river and spread out to dry on a flat rock. We also visited the cliffs where the Caribs, rather than surrender to the French, jumped to their deaths.

We went for a meal one night to a restaurant called Mamma's, and were treated to a meal of West Indian speci-alities including armadillo, manicou (possum), sea urchins, turtle etc. also breadfruit and sweet potatoes. The meal was tasty enough but I decided the armadillo were best left to shuffle about the woods and the turtles in the beautiful tur-quoise Caribbean Sea. The possum definitely delight the eye more than the palate and I shall be happy to leave them all in peace. Apparently we later learned that old Mamma of Mamma's died last year and an article in the local paper announced that she had just been re-interred according to her last request. As I understand it in her fishpond. I could be wrong. It definitely set me wondering about all manner of details, not least of which is what the fish thought of it.

Most of the week I was bumbling around with my eye bandaged up and feeling very unsteady and vulnerable. The gutters in St Georges, even for the well sighted, are a snare and a trap being often two feet deep and eighteen inches wide. No concessions whatever being given to safety. They are of course made to cope with the intense tropical downpours common in this region.

Reverting to the subject of Caribs, one cannot feel too much sympathy for them. The Caribs were very fond of raiding Arawak villages killing the men, capturing the women and eating the boys after emasculating them and fattening them for a spell. They took very poorly to enslavement and often died at an early age from overwork. Slaves reckoned that one imported African was equal to four Caribs.

We met Agincourt who we had last seen in Lanzarote. Oddly enough it doesn't seem strange to bump into folk three thousand miles from where you last met. The trade wind route is long but very narrow.

Our next port of call was Cariacou. After threading our way in through the reefs and about sixty other boats in almost pitch black we dropped anchor in Tyrrel Bay. It was a bit hairy and Lill had a splitting headache, as her allotted job was reef spotting from the bowsprit. Next day we rowed ashore and went for a walk to explore our surroundings. A sign outside of a little shanty announced 'carvings for sale'. So we wended our way up the path to the house being studied closely meanwhile by the black pig. Outside the house stood a huge cauldron of about forty gallons capacity beside which was a smaller one in which a thick liquid bubbled morosely over a wood fire. Inside a shed, ancient tools and implements could be seen. Relics of a bygone age but probably still in use. The old lady showed us a couple of crudely carved boats but declined to have her picture taken saying "no suh, I too ugly". In truth she was no princess but had a most interesting face deeply seamed by experiences during the passing of many years. We waved goodbye and left here amongst the chickens scratching in the yard overseen by a magnificent old rooster.

On the way up to Cariacou we had passed the famous 'Kick em Jenny', a rock around which the currents are so vicious that ships feel they are being kicked around the ocean. However we gave 'Kick em Jenny' a berth of three miles and got away with a couple of playful taps from her big toe. We were hard on the wind the whole trip and not sorry to get into the lee of Cariacou where a three masted barque lay at anchor in Saline Bay.

22nd January. The captain rose early at 06.30 making coffee for the astonished crew and by 07.50 we had weighed anchor and were off into a stiff breeze for Saltwhistle Bay on Mayero but first having to call at Union Island to clear into the next few islands. We found out that it was 'Discovery Day' and the town office was closed so walked to the airport and joined two long queues to see the Customs and Immigration officers who sat side by side! Then off to Palm Island formerly Prune Island but having become devoid of prunes is renamed Palm Island. Palm Island is low lying and covered in palms with not a prune in sight and on its magnificent white beach you almost expect to see dusky figures stewing someone in a large pot. After lunch, up with the anchor and off to Saltwhistle Bay which was plainly visible. We arrived at 15.30 and Else dived to check the anchor, this was our routine on anchoring anywhere. The bay was crammed with yachts which detracted somewhat from its idyllic crescent shape fringed with palms through which one could see the Atlantic breakers thundering onto the beach on the other side of the neck of land one hundred yards away. Played Bobby McClouds tapes of Scottish music all night. Nick like I could keep neither his feet nor his hands still so the cabin resounded with slaps and thumps on thighs and bellies.

23rd January. Off to Becquia today. We have to bypass several islands and the Tobago Cays due to time schedule. Very breezy and plenty of spray coming aboard. Would have been too rough to anchor in the Tobago Cays that are very exposed. Dropped anchor at 15.00 and held first time. Bequia is the last bastion of whaling in these parts done from open boats, which are designed for this purpose. A scamp of a lad asked to look after the dinghy when we went ashore darkly hinting that there were boys about who might pinch something. Thinking there was probably one not far away we settled for $5EC. When I said that I thought he was very expensive for an hour, he shrugged and said "well dat is de price". After a brief look around Admiralty Bay with its open market and the sea edge ablaze with colour, mostly clothes but also gorgeous necklaces worked from coral. Then the covered fruit market mostly run by Rastas who if they were not actively serving anyone adopted a horizontal position on one of the benches. Imagine that in Stockport market!

After a few drinks we had dinner in the 'Whalebone Inn' where the entrance is comprised of the jawbone of a humpback whale and the seats inside are made from its vertebrae. The bar is also a jawbone about twelve feet long. We had a rather good curry chicken, as they would say in the West Indies, for which we had to wait an hour whilst it was cooked from scratch. During this time we had several whiskies and were entertained by a steel band. Slightly befuddled, we paid off our boy and shoved off the dinghy into the darkness making a blind stab as to the direction of *Ospray* but helped by our masthead light, which we had left lit for this purpose. There is quite a history to this island – the original white descendants being from North America on whaling boats, from Scottish farms, French freebooters and Africans. There are supposed to be many fair skinned locals.

24th January. A whole day exploring the shops! Women's unbounded interest in clothes and particularly t-shirts is a constant source of amazement to me. After two hours of this I jibbed and like Mr and Mrs Ramsbottam went off seeking further amusement which I found in a chandlers where I paid dearly for two snap hooks to replace the bent ones on the dinghy hoists. I also went into the Bequia bookshop, which is renowned for its collection of maritime books. We also visited two workshops where beautiful wooded model boats which are made from wood from a gum tree. A row of men sat working on various stages of the boats using only hand tools and broken glass. We were told that it takes about two weeks to complete a boat. I have a fancy to have a go at one, maybe a Spray. For our last night aboard with Paul, Lill and the twins, we bought T-bone steaks and a bottle of Champagne. I gave them a T-shirt each painted with *Ospray's* logo as a memento of their voyage on *Ospray*.

25th January. Up early and by 08.30 we were saying goodbye to Bequia, the whaling town where outboard engines and inflatable dinghies are almost local currency. After a brisk but pleasant sail we arrived at St Vincent and tied up to a mooring by Young Island and arranged via VHF with Charlie Tango and guided to it by the occupant of a boat who came out a mile to meet us. He was a person I would rather not have met in the dark having the somewhat evil visage with many missing teeth, which may have accounted for his imperfect command of the English language.

After an hour, my son Andy and his girlfriend Tracey, who live in Australia, were spotted on the jetty and the dinghy was sent to bring them out to *Ospray*. It was grand to see Andy after nearly five years. A lot of catching up to do. We had a drink at the Lime 'N Pub before getting back to the boat. Then after introductions and a cuppa we went ashore for lunch and to bid farewell to the Quesnels. Copious tears from Else and Lill. Then Else went along to see them to the airport. Andy looks very well on his years down under and Tracey fits in well.

Chapter 7

My Son Andrew and his
Girlfriend Tracey join us for a Spell

28ᵗʰ Janauary. Andy set to work to restow all the stuff on deck and I must say effected a certain improvement. He always was good at organising. My ankle is badly infected and quite swollen developing into an ulcer, this was from a coral scratch while trying to clear the snagged anchor in Trinidad. Else dressed it every day and cleansed it with hydrogen peroxide. No swimming for some time. I decided to rest my foot to hasten the day when I could swim again so I was grounded for a spell while the others went in to explore Kingstown. They walked around town to the fruit and fish markets bringing back some lovely kingfish. Andrew used all his chef's skills to produce the most delicious meal we've had for a long time. The fish was cooked in a tamarind sauce and there was a salsa of mixed vegetables, a salad and a spicy rice dish with cinnamon, mace and raisins.

The next day we headed north to Wallilabou Bay. This was the first time that we tied up to a coconut tree, which is commonly done in the Caribbean but only dreamed about in Britain where coconut palms are seldom encountered. One puts the bow anchor down until it bites while reversing to a handy distance to tie up to a convenient coconut palm. We were delighted to see an old friend come in, *Easy*, another Spray last seen in the Canaries. In the afternoon, the crew left me to walk with their guide Julian to the waterfall with soap and shampoo. They saw grapefruit, cocoa, nutmeg and tons of bananas along the way. After a delicious dip and hair wash standing under the tumbling cold water they returned to the boat having bought a stem of green bananas and some grapefruit along with a quantity of green peppercorns. That night we went out for a lovely meal to 'Ashtons' with steel band music that helped down quantities of cold beer. We left when the music finished.

The entrance to Wallilou Bay is marked by a curious rock formation like Marble Arch. I meant to contrive a photograph of *Ospray* taken through it but didn't get round to it. A bit like Herbert Pontin's picture of the *Discovery* through the mouth of the cave in the Antarctic.

30th January. Off to St Lucia today. In view of the wind direction we opted for Soufriere rather than Vieux Fort. Soufriere is on the west coast north of Grande Piton which along with Petit Piton which is not very petit but merely slightly less grand. The two stand out for many miles away as great volcanic cones thickly clothed with forest where the rock is not too steep but with great sweeps of craggy cliff. Altogether an imposing sight. Once more we tied up to a coconut tree at 17.30 and once more having to stop quarrelling amongst rival boat boys vying for the job of tying our line to a tree!! This was one of the incidents that marred our Caribbean experience. This is a very pretty anchorage, totally sheltered from the northeast trades by a headland and we anchored in tranquil water close to our tree near to the beach.

The beach was lined with coconut palms between which are local boats the construction of which we have never seen before. A log of wood is shaped roughly like a boat then hollowed out by tools and fire, then hot rocks and water to steam the timbers and allow it to be spread open then a wide plank each side with strong frames and gunwales with thwarts and a strong double rowing position. When I asked how the boats were constructed, I was told, *"you take de tree and you cut him to shape, den you got to give him de fire man. Den you got to give him de hot water with de rocks to make him stretch open"!* These boats row extremely well and the oars are always crude but effective instruments in at least two pieces composed of a branch or pole and a piece of flat board wired on to it. We were met two miles offshore by one of the boat boys in one of these craft and it kept up with

170

Ospray doing four knots. His oars bent like canes as he lay into them and he was ready to take our line ashore and claim his $10EC. The price is going up as we travel north. We have since found out that this is something of a sprat to catch a mackerel and that the line tying often leads to a guarding job, maybe a couple of days by taxi round the island all of which the boys would organise for a cut. Some of the boys are extremely pleasant, others are an abomination. They quarrel, curse and resort to thinly veiled blackmail especially with regard to guarding your dinghy.

We visited the 'Hummingbird' restaurant which after all was only twenty yards from the jetty where we had a very fair steak after crab back starter and plenty of wine and very good service indeed. Back to the boat and paid off our boat boy which was a bit superfluous as the jetty and the restaurant entrance was guarded by a large and sinister black man who gave me quite a fright as he blended in with the dark bushes. So I only noticed him when his face was only about two feet from mine. A large scotch and soda on board soon settled my nerves and I fell into a deep sleep, dreaming as I often do, that old Misty was alive and well again! Misty, my old spaniel had died when I was in the Canaries.

31ˢᵗ January. Awoke to the sound of cocks crowing. Into Soufriere to clear and buy odds and ends. Soufriere is a most attractive little town. A painter's paradise full of quaint little buildings set round a tree-lined square with a church on one side. There is a definitely French inflection to the architecture. I was approached by a man on the street who asked me "*you looking for something my friend*"? There was a certain inflection to his voice, which left me in little doubt that <u>whatever</u> I was looking for could be provided. A youth sidled up to Andrew who was walking only slightly ahead of his girlfriend and whispered "Do you like girls"? Andrew said yes he did but at the moment was well provided for. A born diplomat! After a long search and re-directing from helpful people, I managed to buy a couple of films out of which I had run – to use a Churchillian form of phrase.

We had arranged with a local taxi to take us on a mini tour. So off we went to the sulphur springs. As one enters the valley one becomes very much aware of a powerful sulphurous smell. On turning the corner great gouts of steam could be seen belching from the hillside in various places and heavy deposits in yellow sulphur covered rocks. A stream with evil looking black water steamed its way down the valley. The centre part where most activity took place is called the cauldron and apparently the crust of earth is so thin as to not bear walking on and only a year before a guide had fallen through and suffered hideous burns before being pulled out.

Next on the agenda was the mineral baths installed by Louis XVI for the comfort of his troops. The way to these was through the botanical gardens full of beautiful plants and tall trees including immortelle with its brilliant red flowers and mahogany. The baths were small but full of clear water naturally heated from volcanic springs and I stripped off and hobbled in while Else held my bandaged foot clear of the water. The position was not the most comfortable but the water was delicious. Then back to Ben's taxi and the boat.

Agincourt arrived just as we were leaving so we stayed on for a few minutes and swapped stories before pushing on to Marigot Bay where we dropped anchor in the lagoon. This is where Dr. Doolittle was filmed and would like many other West Indian anchorages be delightful, if it were not for so many boats. Don't we spoil the places we like best?

1st February. I spent an easy day idly fishing over the side catching numerous small fish intended as bait. The quiet day was intended to give my foot chance to heal and thereby hopefully hastening my return to swimming and walking. During the afternoon *Agincourt* came in, Andy invited them over for a bar-b-que on deck. Andy's chicken dish and delicious salad went down a treat along with several litres of wine brought by Barry and Jill from the Canaries. A good night swapping stories, playing the accordion and a bit of a singsong. Tumbled into bed slightly owlish to saw the least. This is the lagoon that is hard to see from the sea in which the English fleet hid, disguising their masts as palm trees, while the French fleet sailed right past the bay without seeing them. The English chortled for years about this and as a matter of fact I still do.

Into Rodney Bay before sundown, the inner lagoon is hard to see from even a few hundred yards off shore but by dint of watching someone else go in we found the entrance. As the vicar on honeymoon remarked *"such a delightful little spot and so cleverly concealed"*.

3rd February. Else is now dressing Tracey's foot, which is looking a bit 'crook' after an infected mosquito bite. Attending to Else's bum which has developed a salt-water boil requiring my attention as DIY may well result in sticking plaster on the mirror. At dusk we had a zip round the restaurants and as often happens came back to the first one. Had a lovely meal on crab backs and pepper-pot and returned to the boat with the tree frogs going full pelt and so to bed.

4th February. To the bank to get more cash, then anchor aweigh for Martinique. Ooh la la! I had entertained hopes of a good sail today but as we turned the corner in the islands, we still required both jibs and engine to keep a decent speed up as the wind is still only a few points off the nose. We arrived in the large bay of 'Cul de sac Marin' with good light which was fortunate as this bay is bestrewn with banks and reefs and the way is tortuous indeed. We went ashore and after some time found a restaurant named 'The last Resort'. Undoubtedly meant as a joke but as the evening wore on began to have a ring of truth.

5th February. Andy has received some disturbing news that his partner has broken his leg and the business is in danger of collapse. Always something! Andy cooked the most delectable pasta. We could all have eaten tons of it!

6th February. We up anchored and headed across to Marigot Du Diamant, which we failed to find despite Henry. Then headed out past HMS Diamond Rock which was once called HMS Sloop of war as the British navy hauled guns up to the top of this enormous 600 foot rock with which they pounded the French shipping passing between them and the mainland of Martinique. Until eighteen months later they were starved into surrender but immediately exchanged for French prisoners of the English because of their 'gallantry'. After a lunch time anchorage in Anse Noir, a tiny palm fringed bay we continued to Anse a l'Ane catching a 5lb Blue Runner which needless to say we had for supper with an exquisite sauce by Andy. The anchorage was delightfully quiet while round the corner we could see a forest of masts.

A man on the beach is garbed in a blue apron, white straw hat and blowing a conch shell, obviously selling something, so must needs investigate. Of course he is selling fish, anything up to eighty pounds in weight, any cut you like of wahoo and tuna.

7th February. Awoke to the crowing of a multitude of cockerels. All vying with each other for supremacy of voice. This is not all that entertaining at 05.30 but at 03.30 it can be downright irritating. It reminded me of my ex-neighbours short sighted cock who crowed whenever someone turned the bathroom light on. I wished they would all have a greaseproof paper overcoat for Christmas – or even sooner. Later in the day I relented, I like chickens really and in the West Indies, one seldom goes far without a hen or two and a magnificent rooster scratching around, a bit like England was forty years ago. Doesn't the soul profit from seeing a hen busily scratching the earth and from the fierce golden eye of a cock bristling his cape as he stalks round his harem. I digress.

Off for Fort de France on the ferry today. The town is most decidedly French with patisseries showing displays of elaborate confections enough to make anyone's mouth water. Let alone a mariner with a sweet tooth since he was diagnosed diabetic and not to eat such things!!! Andrew bought a waistcoat from Peru! It is a trifle avant guarde but suits him. The folk in Martinique certainly do have a dress sense and altogether we loved the island. There is a cultural uplift from the English, which I hate to admit and the folk in general seem more refined. Then back to the boat, an egg curry and to bed.

8th February. We decided to head for St Pierre today; the town was totally destroyed in 1902 by a colossal eruption from Mount Pelee who broods above the town in swirling mists. Grumblings were feared from the volcano several days earlier. Many citizens of the 20,000 population wanted to leave but the mayor coming up for re-election and wanting as many votes as possible, refused to make arrangements and shortly afterwards the mountain blew its top and wiped out all but one man, who was at the time imprisoned in a deep dungeon and escaped with his life, badly burnt. Even the ships in the harbour were burnt to the water line before they could get under weigh. One ship alone escaped and arrived in St Lucia with one badly burnt sailor and lots of dead because of the noxious fumes. Many of the ruins are still as they were after the holocaust. Many others have been incorporated into the new buildings. The town was apparently very beautiful and often referred to as 'Le Petit Paris'. The locals are friendly and intelligent with the usual Martinique or French flair for clothes.

That night we heard a band playing in town a quarter of a mile away. The music was West Indian with a compulsive drumbeat and an unusual component, which intrigued me. Gradually the others drifted off to bed and I stayed up long tapping my feet. In the end I could stand it no longer and about midnight I slipped the ties on the dingy and went ashore to satisfy my burning curiosity. I found that the band was a four-piece affair, a guitarist whose efforts I could not hear. Two drummers with different sized tom-toms between their knees, which they beat with fingers and thumbs, and the heels of their hands, so cleverly as to make them almost talk. However, the star of the group was of all things a flautist. He played the melodies with such enthusiasm and an amazing accompaniment of trills and riffs in the manner of a trad jazz clarinettist as to make the hairs on the back of my neck tingle. I rowed back to *Ospray* with these magnetic sounds still making my flesh tingle. I was almost back to the ship when they started up again and I lay awake until they finally ceased. While high above the town Mont Pelee's dark and brooding mass could be seen dimly in the clouds.

10th February. Set sail for Dominica at 11.00. The church bells had awakened us yesterday but now as we left behind this pretty little town all was a bustle on a working day. Further along the coast lay another much smaller village with pretty red roofed houses nestling in every fold of the valley and above the village a multihued patchwork quilt of green. Tiny squares of cultivated land between clumps of trees on the lower slopes of the mountain. In the centre of the village in pride of place stood a small but beautiful church. The whole scene was so tranquil I was minded strongly of a song the Inkspots used to sing. The Three Bells about the birth, marriage and death of Jimmy Brown.

As we emerged from the wind shadow of the mountain, the wind blew strongly but we were so close hauled that we kept the engine on. I confess I am no purist any-way but the pace is also dictated by the need to arrive in good light to avoid the numerous reefs in the Caribbean. Many yachts are wrecked each year. We were two miles south of Scott's Head on Dominica when I saw the whale! In a choppy sea I saw 200 yards off the starboard bow the white fin of a sperm whale. At first I thought it might be the splash of a dolphin. Shortly after and much closer I saw it again followed by the curve of an enormous rippling back. I was electrified and shouted, *"whale off the starboard bow"*, in the very best traditions of Moby Dick! The crew in a fever of excitement all ran forward with cameras as we drew nearer to this vast creature blowing peacefully every few seconds. From the shape and direction of the spout curved and to the left, I knew this to be a sperm whale and he was a big one. We were obviously going to pass very close to him and I darted below to get my video camera. As I went down Else shouted, *"Cut the engine"*, *"We are going to hit him"*. I banged the engine into neutral and came up clutching the video to find the other three peering over the port rail on the bow. Passing within feet of the bow, he had dived without haste and Else said she had a clear view of his huge block shaped head and all the folds and creases of the ridges on his back toward the tail. We were left numb but not speechless with excitement and full of a profound sense of privilege at being allowed to see to a limited degree and share the same environment with such a magnificent beast. That night we all drank a toast to him and to all his kind. Little did we expect to see one so close to land?

We came to anchor just south of Roseau at 'The Anchorage' where a local lad with a pleasant face by the name of James tied us to a concrete post on the beach. This lacked the romance of a palm tree and we felt slightly miffed but all the good palm trees were in use.

11th February. We had arranged an afternoon's outing with a taxi driver named Octavius but went by the name of Sea Cat. He was extremely verbose and kept up a non-stop commentary on all that we passed, every so often he would stop the cab and George his assistant would leap out, disappear into the undergrowth or someone's garden and emerge clutching some exotic fruit or nuts which we were offered with instructions on exactly what it was and how to eat it. The first stop was the botanical gardens where we saw groves of citrus of all kinds, many beautiful plants including an enormous tree with massises trailing roots hanging from its spreading branches. Sea Cat who is definitely an extrovert demonstrated his ability to imitate Tarzan by swarming up a root and swinging from one to another with loud cries. In the park were the smashed remains of a bus under the trunk of a large tree blown down by hurricane David.

Next on the tour was the sulphur springs high up in the mountains when we were caught out in a torrential downpour and sheltered under the same tree as a local with a cutlass in his hand and a large bunch of bananas on his head. The sulphur springs were quite impressive, great gouts of steam arose from the dense rain forest. One small pool was actually boiling and Sea Cat threw a small stone into it, which was followed seconds later by a violent eruption of water and gas, for the entire world as if the forces within resented such intrusion. Meanwhile all round grew all manner of wild fruits on the edge of the forest. Near the boiling pool two bamboo pipes delivered hot and cold water which by manipulation the position of the pipes delivered water of variable temperature into a third bamboo pipe under which one bathed or did one's washing all for free. There must be an enormous potential for generating cheap electricity but I don't know that it is made use of, though up in the mountains is a boiling lake, which though being three hours walk each way we did not see.

However an even greater treat was in store! Off we went swinging along the incredibly bad and winding mountain trails through the dense forest along steep banks with rocky rivers beneath. Sea Cat all the while between crash stops for fruit grabbing, gabbling away until we reached a spot where we parked the bus. A long steep walk in the steamy heat brought us eventually to a sharp bend round which we were suddenly confronted by a breath-taking spectacle. From a cleft in the mountain high above us poured a great waterfall, the thunder of which we could dimly hear from half a mile away. The rest of the way, Sea Cat informed us and I could plainly see, involved fording a torrent by skipping on the boulders one or two of which involved a considerable jump then a long and tortuous climb up the mountain scrabbling over huge boulders and tree roots to a high pool. At first I was going to stay behind because of the pain in my foot, which by now was throbbing heartily. However Else did not want to see me miss out and persuaded me to go which was not hard as I was already sick of missing out on things. Crossing the stream I jumped the biggest gap and felt a tearing pain in my ankle, which was bordering on the unpleasant and kept me quiet for a few moments. While we clambered up the trail through the forest, climbing over huge rocks some as big as houses hearing all the time the increasing roar of the falls until at length there was below us a mighty cataract dropping for its final 80 feet or so over a series of ledges into a large green pool.

The rocks on the left hand side of the falls were streaked with red ochre whilst the right hand side were green with algae and moss. The reason for this is amazing. The water in the falls comes from two different sources. One is hot and the other cold so we swam through the limpid waters of the green pool and sat on a left hand ledge luxuriating in a shower so hot as to be, at first, unbearable. The weight of water pounding your body giving a vigorous massage then like a sauna, the higher up you go the hotter it gets. Gradually we moved up the ledges some of which were conveniently shaped like armchairs until after an hour or so we came to another pool fed only by cold water and into this we plunged with an electric tingle until we were cool again. Then back down again swapping sides from cold to hot. Sea Cat all the while giving Tarzan like yells of exuberance while standing in the most dangerous places and disappearing under the thundering cascades of water. He does this almost every day and says he never tires of it. The West Indians are very clean folk and never lose a chance for a wash. Never once on crowded buses and markets was there a whiff of stale sweat.

Having fortified ourselves with a rum punch and fried chicken at a roadside tavern we were driven along a mountain road alongside of which were plantations of grapefruit trees. Tons of grapefruit lay rotting on the ground. George and Sea Cat true to form jumped out of the bus and came back seconds later with t-shirts bulging with 25 big grapefruit. A sad sight this and puzzling one. Apparently the price of grapefruit is not worth the picking and in Roseau, you can buy ten for $1EC about 20 pence. And this is in a world supposedly hungry for healthy foods. Continuing on our way, we soon entered dense rain forest where the bus was parked and we were led down a jungle track between tall trees with tropical birds calling all round until half an hour later we came to the Emerald Pool. What a sight! A perfect jewel indeed. Lying at the foot of an 80 foot waterfall surrounded by three sides by cliffs on the sides and the top of which great tropical plants and trees some with huge leaves like elephant ears, the reflection of these on the water giving the pool it's name. In the fading light of early evening there was something distinctly Jules Vernish about the scene. Sea Cat stripped down to shorts and climbing 20 feet up the walls leapt into the pool with a loud yell. We all followed but more timidly from the side. The water was deliciously cool and beneath the falls you could scarcely stand under the weight of water. We retraced our steps through the forest in the dark, the birds now silent but the air vibrant with the *kleep kleep* of the tree frogs. On the drive back to the boat we stopped off for more fried chicken and another rum punch and so to bed.

12th February. In the morning Else and Tracey had booked a diving course at the hotel pool. The afternoon was to be a sea dive followed by an hour or two whale watch. So at 13.30 we all climbed into the dive boat, which was a large pirogue with David the diving instructor and Fitzroy the leader who was something of an expert on whales. Fitzroy said if we were lucky we might see a shark. I said *"Lucky?"* Down the coast we went to the tail of the island where we anchored on a patch of sand amongst reefs. I had decided to push my luck and have a dive so Andy and I were rigged up with tanks. Our dive was to be on the edge of the Abyss a deep trough that plunged down over a thousand feet into blue nothingness. A short swim brought us to the edge of this mighty chasm and after 50 feet we peered over the edge into the blue void beneath us. Fish of all colours swam around us and below us we could see larger fish. As the fish increased in size with the depth imagination began to play a part in wondering what may be just out of sight beneath us. David urged us over the edge of the Abyss and we swam round pinnacles of rock swarming with fish before ascending the reef where in 30 to 40 feet we swam over myriads of species of coral. Some of the brain corals were as big as cars and quite fantastic. The site for the ladies dive had been selected as the champagne pool. So having been likewise togged up with all the gear Else, Tracey and an American lady named Donna each in turn went over the side backwards. I was eager to see how Else was enjoying her first dive so I donned a mask and fins. I could see Else was in her element so off I went to look at the champagne pool. I should be getting used to weird and wonderful sights by now but once more I was stunned by the sight which now lay before me. Thousands of glittering strings of bubbles arose from the bottom of the sea for all the world like diamond necklaces swaying in the currents. The sea suddenly became warmer by about 20 degrees. The bubbles were steam issuing from fissures in the rock from an undersea volcano. It was indeed like swimming in champagne! I turned underwater to face the afternoon sun and the effect was electrifying, the whole sea was lit up by a million crystal chandeliers as the sun's rays caught each bubble.

With all the girls back in the boat after their first dive, chattering like magpies about what they had seen, we went for a spell of whale watching. We had hardly gone half a mile when Fitzroy's eyes narrowed and we followed his gaze out to sea. A spout! A large sperm whale was blowing the characteristic spout forwards and to the left! David took the boat to within 500 yards of him and cut the engine in order to drift down gently to the great beast without alarming him. Soon we could see the blowhole as his vast back rolled over like some gigantic tyre and we could hear the organ pipe sound of his breathing. Everyone in the boat was tense with excitement and cameras clicked and whirred as we drew closer. Suddenly when we were within 200 yards of him, a pair of vast flukes reared high into the air as the leviathan sounded. The legendary 'Hand of God' as the old whalers used to say. We were speechless!

These creatures feed at depths down to 3000 feet on giant squid. The contents of sperm whale stomachs indicate that some of the squid are of unbelievable size having tentacles thicker than a man's body. What a day. A life times longing to see a sperm whale and I see nine in three days. I shall never forget the awesome majesty of those flukes that could have smashed our boat to fragments. I slept well and dreamed of whales for months.

13ᵗʰ February. Up early to take Donna to the hotel for her course as she had slept on *Ospray* as no transport could be found. Then I rowed out to a dugout canoe from which three men including a Carib Indian were seining ballyhoo from which I bought a bucket full, these little bright silver fish are excellent bait. We motored down to the south of the island off Scott's Head hoping to see a whale while we fished. Alas no whale and no fish. We motor sailed up the coast to Castaways beach resort.

14ᵗʰ February. Went to Roseau for our mail and to clear customs. Our taxi took us through a couple of villages of extreme quaintness. The tiniest of tiny shacks, some beautifully kept and some plain as plain. Chickens everywhere as usual. What would happen or will happen in the next hurricane. Only the Lord knows. I can see a whirlwind of bits of timber and corrugated iron. We had a good walk around Roseau, stocked up on medical supplies at the excellent pharmacy and then went for a cold drink as it was sweltering hot. On the walk to Customs on the edge of town I bought an enormous grapefruit and six lemons for $1, about 20 pence. We cleared Customs and then caught a drop taxi to Castaways.

Tonight being Valentines night there was a jump up at Castaways and Else and I decided to risk the meal on the assumption that up was the only way such quality could go (Andy put in a complaint about last night's meal). All was not well at the camp; a tiff had developed into a sulk so we made arrangements for Andy to collect us from the jetty on the signal of a whistle. However after a good meal and a bit of a knees up *Ospray* was deaf to all signals. So Else stripped off just beating me and dived into the water to swim for the boat. On the way a shoal of tiny fish left the water in a panic. Naturally she wondered of what they were frightened!

15ᵗʰ February. We refuelled and took on board ice at Prince Rupert Bay and then sailed for Isles des Saintes. We had a glorious sail with the wind just forward of the beam in quite a boisterous sea. Else was feeling poorly with a sore throat and temperature so she went to sleep down below. As we had good visibility and a commanding breeze I elected to take the shorter but more hazardous passage. Passe des Dames was beset liberally on either side by reefs. Every few moments it would erupt in a smother of foam nearly giving me a heart attack. I called Else on deck, poorly or not, as she has sharp eyes and for the next twenty minutes until we were through the dragon's mouth and the thunder of the reefs was behind us. Eyes peered like lasers for the looming rocks beneath the vessel.

Half an hour later we sailed round Le Pain du Sucre and into the Bay of Bourg des Saintes. A very pretty well kept little town as most of the French West Indian towns are. Else was still feeling unwell so Andy, Tracey and I went ashore for a butchers as they say. Perfectly delightful. An exquisite mixture of French Caribbean culture and architecture. Several scooter hire shops, art galleries and batik shops and good cafes. In the little square by the jetty a row of old men sat yarning and laughing, banging the floor with their sticks to emphasise a point or express mirth. I took a sly picture of one old chap pretending to photograph the monument in the square. He regarded me balefully, unconvinced. As in the other islands the women are very slim and beautifully turned out. The buildings are all in good repair and freshly painted.

16th February. Else is still poorly so three of us went ashore and I lashed out and bought a pair of batik shorts which should cut quite a dash at Shrewsbury baths on a winter's Monday morning. Had a lovely wander round the village, which is alive with colour, flowers and shrubs and the gaily-painted houses rich with gingerbread decoration. I bought a homemade coconut ice cream from a lady with a little cart in the street and it was so delicious that I went back for another for Else.

17th February. Up early for Guadeloupe and the marina just south of Basse Terre about ten miles away. We were offered a slightly dicey berth on the end of a pontoon, which was about ten feet long leaving the front and stern parts of the vessel unsupported in a strong breeze. On one side of us was an expensive gin palace constructed chiefly of tinted glass and on the other side a smart official looking vessel with GUARDIA painted in large letters proclaiming this as a police boat. Andy and Tracey disappeared to town to sort out flights etc and Else and I settled to corned beef and tomato sandwiches. Just as we finished there was a knock on the hull. *"Allo, allo, my 'usband 'e is coming back very soon with is beeg fishing boat"*. The lady was polite and apologetic but made it plain that hubby would not be too pleased to find his berth occupied. Having visions of a large bad tempered trawler man with tattooed biceps and a gutting knife, I prepared to move. It was now blowing strongly and as Else cast off the stern rope the stern blew off the dock, at which I heaved a sigh of relief as the davits had been menacing the gin palace windows. However my relief turned to horror as I looked round and saw my bowsprit swinging rapidly towards the windows of the police boat in front. With little room in which to turn, I gave her a kick astern. Now astern *Ospray* is an absolute sow but forwards she is quite responsive so I rammed her in forward and plenty of revs with the helm hard over. I glanced at Else whose ashen face was a study of wide-eyed horror as we charged forward like a knight in armour with a lance intent on impaling the GUARDIA on our bowsprit, which we had extended by another eight feet. At the last moment the rudder began to bite and the end of the bowsprit swept past the windows of the GUARDIA with inches to spare!

18th February. Motored up to Basse Terre and tied up in a corner of the commercial dock severely frightening a French fisherman who was tied up in front of us by nearly braining him with our anchor on the bow. However I had judged my distance well and we caused only a slight dent in his beret. He came to shake hands with me later, though whether this was an act of forgiveness or an insurance against further accidents I could not make out. *"You stop very good"*, he said.

A walk round Guadeloupe's second city Basse Terre. The French settlers must have been singularly unimaginative as the same place names occur in each French island – Basse Terre, Soufriere (dozens), Vieux Fort and so on, while the Spanish depend almost entirely on the names of Saints. Meanwhile the English apparently suffering from pangs of permanent homesickness are inventive enough to name English Harbour next to Falmouth! Basse Terre is like a seedy run down Fort de France but the women are almost as elegant and well dressed. Only French is spoken even in the travel agents, English was a problem. Someone asked "*Parlez vous anglais?*" "*Je parle francais*", was the terse reply.

We set sail about 17.00 for a night passage to Antigua, which became less smooth as we cleared the north tip of Guadeloupe at about 19.30. The moon had appeared characteristically between clouds and a V shaped gap in the mountains. We were sailing hard on the wind and as the night wore on the seas became more impressive. Andy's pot-au-feu went down very well at about 20.00. By midnight we were taking plenty of water over the bow and about 23.00 the wind increased to gale force and for the first time ever the lee rail was driven under as *Ospray* smashed through the waves almost submarine. Still with staysail and jib and single reefed main which was obviously too much sail for peace of mind in the gusts. However she stood up to it well and within half an hour of a violent rainstorm the seas had dropped somewhat – they rose again later and the wind had fallen back to about F6. At the height of the blow our starboard anchor had broken its lashing and jumped out of its roller and was trying to demolish the bows. Duly harnessed I crawled up to the bow and managed to pull the anchor over the bow assisted by a timely wave, which more or less flung it on deck where I lashed it firmly. Although I was drenched to the skin the water felt beautifully warm so it wasn't too unpleasant. One of the great differences between sailing in the Tropics as against sailing in Scotland.

Approaching pitons of St Lucia with cargo of bananas.

Off for a snorkel!

Moored to a coconut tree!

"The Hand of God".

My son Andrew.

Carib fishermen in Dominica.

Valentines night at Castaways Hotel, Dominica.

Rainbow in Guadeloupe.

Chapter 8

Alone from Antigua!

About 05.00 we could see the lights of Antigua and shortly after this the autohelm went on the blink. Keeping well offshore to avoid the extensive reefs, which reach for several miles, we bashed into the wind and seas having handed the sails at about 06.30. We were not sorry to slide into the relative quiet of English Harbour where we dropped anchor in Nelson's Dockyard. We were delighted to see *Agincourt* anchored a short distance away and all fell into a fitful sleep after a long stressful night.

19th February. After due formalities and a cold drink ashore we went aboard for a lunchtime siesta much needed after last night. English Harbour is a fine natural harbour capable of holding several hundred vessels. There are perhaps 70 at the moment of which maybe a quarter fly the British colours. Nelson's Dockyard has been restored by the Nicholsen family with some grants. The Nicholsens were on the way round the world from their home in Ireland and saw the decrepit old dockyard and thought it had promise and stayed on. The place is an impressive monument to the British Navy of Nelson's day. The buildings are beautifully designed and built each to its own purpose in supplying and outfitting the ships of the time. The Copper and Lumber store is now an attractive restaurant which at the Bar, on Tuesdays and Fridays, are two-for-one drinks and on Friday, fish and chips in English newspaper. The fish is snapper and not cod or haddock, matters not. Three other bars and restaurants, all part of the old dock complex have a Happy Hour with half price drinks so, starting at 5 o'clock until 8 o'clock you can wander from one to the other and be quite well oiled by the time you have to pay normal price for drinks – especially as every drink is at least a double. Indeed at one bar I couldn't believe my eyes when a tumbler was half filled with scotch on the rocks before the soda went in.

Many of the boats are those of liveaboards who have either found work in Antigua or are just resting for a few months before deciding where to go next. The children of these families have the time of their lives being free to go and come as they please in the boat's dinghy. Many have cobbled up a sailing rig using broomsticks and old sheets etc and twice a week they have races round the harbour. Imagine! Six or seven year olds taking out their own boat and sailing it. The water is warm and they can all swim like fish so where's the harm.

We went several times by bus to St John's the capital at about 12 miles distance. The first time Andy and Tracey came to find out about flights etc. The bus ride itself was quite an experience. The buses hold about twenty people and are usually full often with standing passengers which does not deter the drivers from hurtling round the tiny lanes at break neck speed. I was astounded to get to our destination in one piece and emerged somewhat shakily into the torrid heat of St Johns. Now here is an amazing thing. Although the buses were cram packed full of poor folk living in tiny little houses there was never a hint of sweaty smells though the temperature was in the 90's. The only instance of dirty clothes was I regret to say two English men, both yachties, who distinguished themselves by filthy t-shirts. As usual the school children were sparkling clean, neat uniforms and very well behaved. In fact, the whole of the time we were in the West Indies I never saw one instance of bad behaviour or one instance a teenager swearing – and only very occasionally an adult. The bus stops regularly to let some straw hatted lady off with her bundles of shopping, right at the bottom of her garden path. Some one lifts her bags out to her and off she goes with a cheery smile into her eight foot by ten foot house.

Never in my life have I heard a laugh heartier than the West Indians especially the women. It's enough to make the sphinx laugh! A bus ride is an entertainment. One old lady prodding the driver and going on at him for driving too fast. Threatening to tell his Auntie Sophie and so on. I didn't notice him slowing down though! Others were going on about their love life or someone else's. In every village washing streamed from the lines, hens, cockerels and some fine old roosters pecked in the yard, goats browsed at the roadside, and dogs lounged in the shade. On the porch a West Indian lady in a straw hat sat munching on something or other. The West Indians are voracious eaters even when the temperature stuns the European appetite until the sun sets.

20ᵗʰ February. We must also get down to some more rigging maintenance while Andy is still here to help. They leave on the 24ᵗʰ. We found Yachtronics and the man came out to look at the depth sounder, he may also examine the Cetrek, which is the autohelm, that's not working again. I have installed a new fuse box. Andy and I are being very busy replacing the 'bob' stays with chain. The port one broke when the anchor came loose on the crossing. We also removed the extension bowsprit, tightening the main stays and freeing the windlass. In the evening we went over to *Agincourt* for a drink taking a bottle of white wine. Jill's Mum May is on holiday from England with them. May looks after her mother who is 93, a bit slow on her feet and loosing her eyesight.

23ʳᵈ February. Before Andrew and Tracey left for Australia we went to the Sunday 'jump up' at Shirley Heights in the afternoon by taxi, named after Governor General Shirley whom Nelson did not like. The feeling was mutual, as Nelson would not allow other ships than the English to trade, so enforcing the Navigation Act. Sir Richard Hughes under whom Nelson was stationed, had blinded himself in one eye while chasing a cockroach with a fork. We had better watch it!

There was a bar-b-que to provide chicken, pork and of course hamburgers. At least one and often two steel bands play all day. I find a steel is band compulsive listening and this was no exception. They played with great enthusiasm and skill. We met Barry, Jill and May thoroughly enjoying themselves with their usual gusto. Andy left early to walk down the hill, which didn't look easy so we decided to return by taxi to the boat. Andy cooked us a beautiful though rich supper of pasta and a Caesar salad with a bottle of champagne. He did us proud. Meanwhile Tracey finished her packing and set the alarm clock.

24th February. Up at 05.30 to get the taxi to the airport for 06.30. It was sad to see Andrew and Tracey leave. Back at the boat Trevor from Yachtronics is coming to see if he can help us fix the depth sounder and Cetrek. We had also stopped off at Pumps and Power and they will fill the gas cylinders if there before 09.00. A simple supper of leftovers and a few beers – the boat does feel quiet!

The next month was spent hounding various establishments to honour their promises for swift attention to our request for urgent repairs on various items of equipment essential to our continuing voyage back to the UK. As much as we enjoyed our stay in Antigua this long and frustrating delay meant we had to change our plans to visit Boston and see the eastern seaboard of America. *Ospray* was registered in Boston, (UK) as also emblazoned on the stern of the original *Spray*.

I 'phoned my brother Bryan in Bristol, UK, on his 50th birthday on 2nd March. I have a story to tell about "the lesser of the two weevils". While we were in the Cape Verdes, part of our grocery shopping consisted of packs of pasta. Else decided to have a clear out of the packet cupboard. She discovered the presence of some weevils when she put the bag onto a block in the cockpit. The block and deck were crawling to my horror. I could not believe my eyes as they scurried to hide anywhere at which thought the mind boggled.

A blood-curdling scream drew our horrified attention to a boat mooring next to us. A young girl was handling the anchor chain being winched in and caught her hand in the chain. She fainted on the bow. Else handed a bag of ice to a person rushing to her aid from a nearby boat. Luckily she escaped with severe bruising only.

Warnings of a severe water shortage on the island were issued advising utmost care in unnecessary use. Showers were banned. Shortly after this we observed the crew of a vastly expensive yacht hosing their already immaculate decks down with fresh water. We were disgusted and did not hide the fact.

When we went to clear with Customs and Immigration, there was a very large policeman bearing a close resemblance to Idi Amin who had discovered Else's origins in Trinidad. He leaned forward and said seriously but with a twinkle in his eye, *"Trini, if I find you here after tomorrow, you in big trouble!"*

24th March. Up early and sailed half way up the west coast and dropped the hook in the supposed lee of Maiden Island which is only 100 yards across. Pelicans could be seen roosting in the trees. Flapping wildly from time to time to regain their balance after a gust had dislodged them. We launched the dinghy and went on an exploratory trip to the beach about a mile away. The beach looked firm but we waded ashore through a horrid squelchy mixture of mud and weed no doubt squirming with all manner of loathsome creatures armed with fearful teeth or stings or both. This part of the bay is ringed with mangroves, which no doubt accounts for the murkiness of the water. We found what we thought were turtle eggs, transparent globes the size of ping-pong balls, or a little smaller. Nearby were several big scrapes in the sand that may well have been turtle nests.

BERMUDA

VIRGIN ISLANDS

TORTOLA

ROAD TOWN

VIRGIN GORDA

DORADO

ANGUILLA

ST. MARTIN

SABA

STATIA

ST. BARTS

ST. KITTS

PELICANS

BASSETERRE

ST. JOHN'S

NEVIS

CHARLESTOWN

ANTIGUA

MONTSERRAT

OSPRAY

GUADELOUPE

POINT-A-PITRE

DOMINICA

ROSEAU

FORT-DE-FRANCE

MARTINIQUE

MAY SHE HAVE
FAIR WINDS & CALM SEAS
AND ANY STORMS
BE LITTLE ONES
AND SOON OVER

CASTRIES

ST. LUCIA

ST. VINCENT

KINGSTOWN

BEQUIA

MAYREU

CARRIACOU

WEST
INDIES

ST. GEORGE'S

GRENADA

TRINIDAD & TOBAGO

FLYING FISH

Chapter 9

The Leeward Islands

25th *March*. Up anchor and away for Nevis which we could see in the distance. Shortly after leaving the bay it struck me that we were heading too far south and in fact steering for Montserrat, beyond which we could see the tiny island of Redondo. For three hours we motored due to lack of wind and when as Slocum liked to put it, "*a smart breeze sprung up from the east*". Overcoming the torpor induced by the heat and two breakfasts the first at 06.45 of toast and marmalade and the second at 09.30 of egg, bacon and beans, we got up to raise the jib and staysail. No sooner had we reached the foredeck when the reel screeched and line whizzed away at a fine old rate. I grabbed the rod and was immediately aware that I was fast to a big fish. As he had already taken a couple of hundred yards of line I told Else to follow him. A furious fight ensued. Every time I gained line he would rip it off again very soon. After 20 minutes he surfaced and I could see a large dorado about five feet long weighing perhaps 50 lbs. Shortly after he leapt clear of the water shaking his head with an effort to throw the hook. For another ten minutes after he and *Ospray* circled each other without gaining or loosing line. I had him rolling on the surface. He was unbelievably beautiful. A body as gold as a ray of sunshine, fins of the most exquisite deep blue. Surfeited as I was with a recent breakfast and lacking the tang of hunger essential to keen hunting, I decided to let him go. He was too beautiful to kill. Else leaned over the rail with the net. Just then fate took a hand. Without guidance the boat rolled heavily in the swell, four washboards and Else's bikini bottom splashed into the water on top of the wallowing fish, who finding a last reserve of strength plunged under the boat neatly cutting the line on the keel. He would have been my largest fish ever. Dorado is one of the finest of fish. We retrieved the washboards but alas not Else's bikini.

We came to anchor off a palm-fringed beach north of Charlestown. On diving to check the anchor we found it had dragged for about 30 feet before digging in. I had reversed the engine vigorously and although this is often advocated, I am beginning to think that this is bad practice on many bottoms and that the anchor is best left to be pulled under gradually, before testing it with a good pull, if you cannot dive on it, which is much better but will get few volunteers in northern waters.

A one mile dinghy ride to the pier then a walk through town to the Mariner's Wharf Bar where we had a beef roti and a cold Carib beer and talked to a couple from Alaska on their belated honeymoon. He was a pilot for the Fish and Wildlife Commission and spent his life counting wildfowl and moose and such. He was just now setting up a kayaking business and guarantees his clients a sighting of a least two of the following – whales, eagles, sea lions, porpoise and bears. I told Jack about the Norwegian/American who had fired my imagination about a canoe trip down the Nahani river. Jack knew the area well and said that Juneau where they live is only three hundred miles from the Nahani, which he said was stunningly beautiful and a flight out would cost about US$170. I thought this was an amazing coincidence to be exploited.

I saw a huge turtle swim by the boat; his head was as big as a person's and his body must have been five feet long.

26th March. Clearing customs is rarely a simple job. The place marked Customs sent us across the road to an unmarked building inside which were several unmarked offices, one of which we found to be Customs, where we filled in the usual forms after which we were sent back to the first building to pay more money. From there we were directed to the police station about half a mile away to clear with the Immigration side of things. After this we had to go back to the second building in which a lugubrious lady suffering from toothache told us to come back in two days time for our cruising permit. Exhausted by all this bureaucracy, we staggered into a patio garden café for refreshments but not before arranging with Billy, a taxi driver, who had watched our every movement like a cat watching a mouse, for a trip round the island next day.

27th March. Else's birthday. Up before the sun as it is raining and I wanted to catch some water from the tarpaulin. Two men fishing not far away and several others out on the horizon. Ashore we found that Billy couldn't come and had sent Edmund instead so off we set. We went to the first hotel built in the West Indies, Bath Hotel and Spring House, in ruins but the baths had been kept up, water bubbling up from the floor at 106 degrees F. The baths were built by the Huggins family. One goes down a flight of stone steps where there is a row of shallow tiled baths, very Victorian looking, each with several inches of water from the hot springs. The water felt too hot and would have to be entered very gingerly.

Next was Nelson's museum. He married Fanny Nesbit a Nevitian widow and the museum was full of interesting Nelsonian relics and memorabilia including of course lots of paintings of the sea battles and showing amidst billowing clouds of gunpowder smoke horrific scenes of destruction and carnage. Quite often ships would lock together and blast away till the gunpowder ran out when the colours would be struck. In one battle a ship had only three casualties and one of whom was a sailor who had deserted his post and been stabbed to death by an officer. "*Pour encourager les autres*". No doubt. While Nelson was in Nevis he knocked around with Prince William, his best man, and later to be crowned William 1V. We visited the church in which he was married and saw the marriage certificate. A large fat lizard was sunning himself on the path by the church door.

All along the windy little roads were the wee shanty houses with their little gardens planted with bananas, yams and sweet potatoes and surrounded by flowers of every colour, all bright primary colours. There is little subtlety in the Tropics, which seems right for the area! Edmund then took us to a plantation house, the colonial grandeur of this contrasted sharply with the native dwellings, which were reminiscent of pictures of Uncle Tom's cabin.

We stopped at a local café 'Peto' for chicken and chips and a locally brewed soft drink – ginseng and was delightful. The east coast is very barren, overrun by wild goats and donkeys. They eat all the vegetation and dig up the root crops. Then back along the coast to town where we stopped to see Kennedy, a deaf and dumb young man, who carves birds and fish in a tiny hut. We bought a pelican. Else thought it had a beautifully comical expression and will remind us of the pelicans flying and diving into the sea, something that we often watch and find just as interesting each time. We named our carving 'Kennedy'.

28th March. The island was originally called 'Oualie' by the Arawaks, meaning the island of sweet water, then followed the name given by Colombus of 'Nuestra del las Nieves', Our Lady of the Snows, so called by Colombus as the 3000 foot mountain is usually capped by clouds falling down the sides and looking like white snow. Then the Scottish settlers named the island 'Nevis' after their original highland home close to Ben Nevis.

We saw Edmund, who showed us his house which was being built, very large and of concrete blocks. His wife gave us some potatoes, at least 15 to 20 lbs. A walk around the market buying provisions (as a West Indian would say), and came home with pork and goat neck. We had a last ginseng with Jack and Molly and said goodbye as they are off back to Alaska to spend their time watching and counting grizzlies and moose! We booked a table at the Courtyard – Caribbean Confections.

We had a scrumpscious meal of roast coconut and Tania fritters for hors d'oeuvres, beef stew, roast pork, ginger pumpkin, christophene in a white sauce and cole slaw with lots of coconut. This went down beautifully with a carafe of red wine. Desert was pawpaw cobbler full of cinnamon. A superb setting outside amongst the greenery of a lot of different Caribbean fruit and palm trees. Our table companions were Americans who were very interested in our voyage. They have dwelt here for thirty-one years, long before electricity came to the island.

29ᵗʰ March. While snorkelling in the morning we sighted what we thought could be a turtle, then we decided it was a car tyre, then discovered it was a dead pig – a black one. We also saw a strangely weird looking fish beneath the dinghy in some eelgrass. It looked prehistoric. We later identified it as a type of gurnard. The last dive we made was off the beach where *Ospray* was anchored and we found the wreck of a fairly big sailing vessel. We collected shards of pottery though whether they were from the wrecked vessel, I do not know.

Later we had a barby on the beach with Ken and Chris, a couple who had left dentistry in England for a cruising life. An oil lamp was hung from an overhanging palm tree and a blazing fire soon made from coconut husks of which there was abundance nearby. Our fare consisted of grilled pork chops, salad, baked potatoes and baked beans. Desert and wine care of our guests. The mosquitoes were kept away by the smoke from the coconut husks. We yarned and laughed the hours away with the two dentists. They are planning another year or two in the Caribbean going to Trinidad for the hurricane season then ultimately through the Panama Canal to the Pacific in *Slica*. A happy night. A tiny sketch in my diary of the scene with the lantern hanging from the leaning coconut tree and the fire beneath to remind us, if we needed, of an unforgettable night.

1ˢᵗ April – rabbit, rabbit, rabbit! Last night's supper was goat stew with dumplings and a bottle of Chilean red wine.

The Nordic Prince came in to berth by us to the welcome of a steel band. Fleets of taxis were there to whisk the tourists away on tours. Thousands of them were disgorged coming down the gangways like a swarm of leaf cutter ants.

The Nordic Prince towered over the dock resplendent in her stainless steel and polished glass. I had visions of immaculate waiters and silver service, caviar and champagne on ice. But I'll bet she never tied up to a coconut tree or her clientele dined on home made goat stew and dumplings! The guests on these tour ships often conform to a type – mostly exhibiting at least several of the following characteristics and sometimes all of them – overweight, infirm, elderly, garrulous, noisy and very pale. Few of them seem to be enjoying themselves though some manifest a sort of false hilarity to give the impression that they were having the time of their lives. Quite sad really. One old couple, though, in their late 70's I imagine, walked up the quay with an arm round each other. Else said they may be on their honeymoon. I said maybe they just liked each other still, after all these years, brilliant.

Else burst into the cockpit to my shout that a turtle with a green stripe down his back had surfaced by the boat. She was a bit sniffy when I reminded her that it was All Fools Day.

Thomas the taxi driver took us for an excursion into the island. We drove past fields of sugar cane, some cut and some burned ready to cut. I should imagine that cutting cane in this climate is hellish work. Dirty, dusty and exhausting. Mechanical harvesters are used but many fields are too steep or bumpy and have to be cut by hand. There is an understandable reluctance on the part of the islanders to be involved in this type of work. Resentment from the days of slavery that was only a couple of great granddads away. When I talked about the paucity of jobs in the island, one dusky lad said with startling vehemence, "*I ain't cutting no cane. Dat fo sho*".

First stop was the batik workshop in a magnificent old colonial plantation house. Batik is produced by painting designs on fine Sea Island cotton cloth with molten paraffin wax. The cloth is then dip dyed and only the unpainted cloth takes the dye except that the wax cracks slightly allowing fine lines of dye to show through which is very attractive.

The wax is then boiled off and the whole process is repeated for each different colour required. The girls sat before the cloth, which is stretched on a frame, painting the designs very deftly usually from a pattern but sometimes free hand. No two pieces of batik cloth are exactly the same. Else bought several pieces with which to sew cushions.

We then passed Bloody Bay where thousands of Caribs were massacred by the French. The blood was said to have flowed down the river into the bay for three days. A dreadful event ameliorated only by the fact that the Caribs had been slaughtering the peaceful Arawacks for centuries before this. Those that live by the sword .....

In the first few years following Columbus's discovery, hundreds of thousands of Arawaks and Caribs were slaughtered by the Spanish in pursuit of converting them to Christianity!! Slow garrotting, burning alive and many other products of the Spaniard's fruitful imagination were used to persuade the wretched Indians that Jesus loved them! Many Spaniards did not believe that Indians and black men possessed a soul, therefore could not be counted as human beings and considered a quick death as a merciful act.

Back to the tour. Fort George on Brimstone Hill, a monumental fortress 800 feet high with revetments and gun positions at every level. This mighty defence took slaves 100 years to build and became known as the Gibraltar of the West Indies. From this position the English, with a force of 1000 men, held out for a year against 800 French before running out of food and an honourable surrender, whereby the officers were sent back to England, no doubt to step straight onto another ship and rejoin warfare with their captors. What an age of chivalry! Cannon are everywhere arranged along all the battlements and revets but also used as gateposts etc. The large 18 to 24 pounders probably weigh two or three tons each. Moving these up the steep slopes must have produced much sweat from man and horse. From this elevation a large area could be commanded by cannon fire giving a huge advantage over a besieging ship whose guns would have to be elevated at crazy angles in the hope of landing a lucky shot.

Lastly a visit to a sugar factory where cane is made into sugar. The factory was large and noisy with steam and smoke hissing and belching from numerous places and the roar of heavy machinery all but drowning out the shouts of the workers operating the plant. Our guide at a range of a few inches had difficulty in making himself heard. Basically some hundred of tons of cane are firstly crushed in a series of giant shredding machines that release much of the sugary sap. The broken fibres travel a conveyer belt and are washed then vacuum dried before being fed into the boilers as fuel to be devoured into the roaring furnace. The syrup is then concentrated in huge pressure cookers before the sugar is crystallized out and bagged for export.

3rd April. Yesterday we ended up having sunburned backs and legs from snorkelling all day long. This morning Else was in the cockpit when she spied a boat approaching our stern at a rate of knots. There was a resounding crash and I heard Else's loud cry of protest and rushed on deck to assess the damage. An American gent came on deck and apologetically said. "*What a hell of a way to introdoos yourself!*" He had been handling the anchor while his wife had slipped the engine into forward instead of astern. We settled the matter amicably with US$100 changing hands. I managed to repair most of the damage to a tolerable state. No fuss, no court proceedings, the best way.

We were soon sailing past Brimstone Hill and Mount Misery and are just at the end of the island. The wind is a bit fluky from behind but we've just got the two jibs up and no engine. There was a slight tug on the line and quite easily a small barracuda was brought in. Else had strict instructions to keep those sharp teeth away from me – sans vestments! A flick of the tail and he was away to the depths. Twenty minutes later there was a much bigger bite taking lots of line. This time a 25lb barracuda which would not fit in the net. He was huge and with even bigger teeth and as soon as the hook was out, returned to the sea. They eat the reef fish, which have ciguatera, a toxic poisoning by accumulation. It affects humans with diarrhoea and vomiting followed by neurological ailments e.g. tingling sensations and joint pains. There is no way to test a fish prior to eating – tuna, dolphin, wahoo, sailfish and marlin are safe.

We had soon covered the 19 miles to St Eustatius (Statia which is Dutch). We anchored bow out to face the swell, and ended up rolling quite a lot. The jetty was bristling with steel reinforced rods sticking out above and below the water line, not a place where you would want to take your dinghy.

4th April. It had been quite a bouncy night and a noisy one. We lost one of our fenders so the dinghy banged the hull till I retied it. Else had previously been up to move the makeshift crowbar that had been rolling around and which she said I had never heard! It was too bouncy to go ashore. We had yesterday's forecast from *Giriz 1*, a high-pressure area centred locally with winds F3-4 from S, SE for 24-36 hours. The swells were building and a few boats had already left. We worried about clearing Customs but didn't, as the other boat hadn't either. But it wasn't so easy just to sail off. The stern anchor was not at the end of the rope! I went over to find it, and when I eventually did, I dived to tie it again. I came up gasping, expecting to have a heart attack. Else, thinking that it had been tied, started hauling. I could see the line disappearing out of the ring and shouted, "*stop*" with all the breath I could muster. Else also saw that we had lost the bow roller and spied it not far away. She tried to dive for the bow roller but found her ears too painful when still 10 foot off the bottom. I had to dive again, and this time managed to get to both. The stern anchor now aboard and the bow roller fixed in place, we both sat down to a well-deserved rest!

Shall we stay or shall we go? On to Saba or head for Gustavia? The waves were no worse but we decided to go. I went below for a well-deserved sleep to recuperate. Some time later Else shouted by name excitedly. She had seen a shape suspended in the air alongside. She thought it might have been a porpoise or a small whale. Looking beneath the water's surface I could see a brown shape and thought it may have been a pilot whale.

Else was sorry that we never went ashore at Statia, to walk up the slave road to the town and then into the crater, the Quill crater some 2000 feet high. The dense rain forest in the crater is supposed to have some of the largest trees in the Leeward Islands, some of the buttress roots being 6-7 feet high.

Soon we were approaching the southeast end of the island. One could see bare cliffs with a town perched high on the top; heaven alone knows how one gets there. Sailing past Fort Bay, there was a tiny harbour, no room for a large boat like us, a steep road snaking up to the town of 'The Bottom'. This is where we should clear with Customs. Passing Ladder Bay, I could see the 800 steps cut into the rock, which joins the road to Bottom. Here I saw about six boats moored some on tourist buoys but we would have to anchor, as there were none vacant. Having a mosey around prior to anchoring, I headed between Diamond and Pilot rocks. There were some quite nasty looking spikes above the water. We also saw some very maliciously, dangerous looking rocks just submerged! About turn and back to anchor in the permitted anchorage, of which there are only two areas around the island. The sea being a National Park.

A check on the anchor, which was well in but the swell managing to lift all of the anchor chain off the seabed! Small fish came to see if any food was being stirred up. So here we are anchored in 30-40 foot of water with cliffs to port, rock falls, one empty looking house high up the hill side, the north west end of the road climbing probably 1:2, and with dainty tropic birds flying overhead joined by the occasional frigate bird.

That evening a dinghy came heading steadily towards us. It was a visit from Jim and Julie, an American couple on their replica of a *Spray*. We chatted into the night, a new moon and thousands of stars twinkling above – what a place.

5th April. I woke early and enjoyed a leisurely read with my cup of 'rosie lee'. Again, my blood sugar count is high, 14 today and 16 yesterday – not sure why, but not good enough. The anchorage is comfortable and a lovely smell of bacon is drifting down wind to us, unfortunately we have none.

We went off to visit *Canores*, Jim and Julie's *Spray* and he later dropped us ashore braving the surf and boulders. We managed to jump out quickly on a small patch of sand. Now for the 800 steps uphill. Half way up the steps there was a picture depicting the landings of ships' tenders. This was the only landing place on the island at that time. Men could only walk up in single file and yet carried provisions, 'a piano and a parson' up the hill. Several stops for a breather later we got to the top of the 'ladder'!

A Dutch lad we met on the beach said it was a five-minute walk into town. He was sweating walking <u>down</u> the steps. He had come over to take his driving and HGV licence, in a place that has hardly any roads and what there is, goes straight up and then down again!

Most of the folk spoke English, as I was worried about trying to understand Dutch, and we soon found somewhere that sold cold drinks. We then made our way from "The Bottom" down a steep winding road to Fort Bay, clearing Customs and paying our dues at the National Park Office next door.

6th April. It is lovely to be able to dive overboard at any time and enjoy a cool swim in the hot and humid weather. Then a leisurely hot drink whilst wrapped in a towel, watching huge Atlantic rollers crashing against the boulders coming from the north. That was a portent of unsettled weather in the north where I know there are gales. There is an osprey hunting above, unlucky so far, and the tropic birds crying *'kree-kree-kree'*.

Susan, from the Dive Office and Marine Park came to warn us that if the swells kept coming from the north, the anchorage would get terrible, waves crashing over Diamond rock. So I decided to move onto one of the spare yellow buoys as it would make get away easier in the morning, when we had planned to leave.

We went for a swim and snorkelling off Torrens Point. There was a mass of elkhorn, brain and other corals, a few sea eggs and millions of fish swimming around us in hues of gold, grey and silver, some with horizontal stripes, some with spots. One fish swam with its dorsal and caudal fins only; it had no ventral fins, and was a dark grey/brown colour with an iridescent blue outline between its body and fins. There were many garfish and small barracudas and I am sure that the trumpet fish followed us.

7th April. Up before 06.00 feeling the change in the wind and it is starting to rain. About twenty minutes later Else had almost filled the two blue containers of water. As it is, the main tank is empty. So shortly after 06.25 we were leaving the north west coast of Saba, heading between the dive buoys and Diamond Rock, standing out white because of the guano from the birds that roost and live there.

There is still plenty of rain about; we are heading directly into the wind, waves and dark rain clouds. We are looking behind at the last of the islands that 'Brush the Clouds' and ahead are the Renaissance Islands, also covered in clouds at the moment. St Barthelemey was French, then Swedish and is now French again. It is all of 6 miles long; you can easily drive around and see the sights in a day. Most things appear to be very conveniently close to the anchorages. Anchoring soon after midday, we then cleared Customs with the Port Captain for two days and found there were letters waiting for us from Lill, Cathy and Hillary. Later we went to find the shell beach. We couldn't believe what we saw – it was inches deep in shells where the tide washes them up! Else's handbag was soon feeling very heavy! Just before 18.00 I saw a Peugeot bike rental place and ordered us one for the next 24 hours. Else is not sure about the forthcoming experience!

8ᵗʰ April. Else thought she should pack a first aid kit for our trip around the island and put in a long roll of plaster and antiseptic cream into her handbag. Just in case! We drove round the island on the inside as Else was lacking in confidence in my driving to go on the outside which is next to sometimes horrific drops. The little scooter did beautifully up all of the hills. The countryside was quite dry, many sorts of palms and low-lying scrub plus the inevitable goat. We walked rocky beaches and saw different corals and even more shells. Getting back to the dinghy, it had been caught under the jetty and required extensive repairs. A job for tomorrow.

9th April. We beached the dinghy for repairs. The bike was returned to Else's surprise undamaged.

10ᵗʰ April. Anchor stowed and motoring out by 07.30. Just a short passage across, about 12 miles to our next stop of St Maarten. I spoke to Bobby's Marina where we had booked a berth for the week that we would be away in Trinidad. Surprise, surprise, Michael whom we had met in Machico, Madeira was also there working in Bobby's Marina. We eventually settled between a cat and a tri – also buying three fenders and three padlocks at a 'hell of a price'.

The plane left early with just a quick stop at St Lucia and arrived in Piarco, Trinidad where Stuart, Else's brother, and his children were waiting for us. Meeting family, the wedding and then all too soon on the 15ᵗʰ boarded flight BW401 and were back in St Maarten.

16ᵗʰ April. There is a lot of interesting gingerbread designs about on the houses. Both Else and I drew some of them in our diaries. The gingerbread would be found in the eaves of the houses, on the balconies, anywhere horizontal or vertical or at an angle. The patterns enhance the appearance of the houses quite dramatically.

I bought a pair of yellow unsinkable binoculars and a camera and the shop assistant offered to take us for a drive tomorrow afternoon, which I eagerly accepted.

17ᵗʰ April. A relaxed morning tidying up the boat, sorting our shopping and making a list of supplies needed for our onward voyage. Prakash came for us about 15.30 and off we went in his left hand drive van, Else sitting on a child's step between the two front seats, holding on for dear life especially when driving round the corners. We spent a lovely afternoon together, sightseeing, swimming at different beaches and on the French half of the island while swimming we could see the lights of Anguilla in the distance. Back on board *Ospray* we chatted about our different lives. Prakash asked me if he arrived in London, would he be picked up at the airport? He also told us about the tourist train arrangements that can be a fantastic way to see India.

That evening we went to a Chinese restaurant and had their special. Our table mats interested us – I was born in the year of the Ox (1937) – *"Bright, patient and inspiring to others. You can be happy by yourself, yet make an outstanding parent. Marry a Snake or a Cock. The Sheep will bring trouble"*. Else was born in the year of the Tiger (1950) – *"You are aggressive, courageous, candid and sensitive. Look to the Horse and Dog for happiness. Beware of the Monkey"*. For our lucky cookies at the end, I had, *"In God we trust; all others must pay cash"*. Else had, *"Your mentality is alert, practical and analytical"*.

The next few days were a haze of shopping, looking at electrical goods and for presents to take back home to the UK. One quiet evening aboard, I was thinking of our pleasant life but also looking forward to fishing and stalking in Scotland and the cool air. Else found it hard to understand that I wished to be in the Highlands instead of the warm tropical surroundings.

22nd April. We motored as we so often did with the wind on the bow. The coastline looks beautiful, soft white sand, cliffs and rocks, some of the houses blending well. Goodbye to Groote Baii and hello to Road Bay.

That night we ate at a French restaurant on the beach, 'Rivera', the table looking out at the breaking swells and a vibrant purple sunset. Walking back to the dinghy we stopped for a while at 'Johno's' where there was live music.

We did not stay long as Else was sad as she had heard that Pops, Paul's father, had died.

Anguilla describes herself as 'Tranquillity Wrapped in Blue'. The mainland is surrounded by a coralline marine habitat. Marine Resource Management Regulations have been set up and say *"Please help us protect our tomorrow today – Just leave your bubbles behind!"*

One of our dinghy trips was to go out to Sandy Island a few miles north of Anguilla with a picnic in the cooler box. We snorkelled round the island, and I had the new underwater camera in hand. It was exciting as the breaking waves and the surging water made swimming difficult. The coral was never far from our bodies, reaching out to snag us. Also the expectation of seeing a barracuda behind with its large staring eyes and sharp teeth! The colours of the parrot fish and purple smiling bluetangs were magnificent and all too soon we had swum round the island and were ready to warm up in the sun.

Chapter 10

Looking Forward to Visiting the Land Famed for its Century's Old Tradition of Swashbuckling Tales of Piracy!

25ᵗʰ April. We left Road Bay by 14.00 heading for Virgin Gorda and it will be our first night passage on our own. We had enjoyed having family with us to share our sailing experiences and see a bit of the world. However since leaving Antigua we have sailed on our ownsome and enjoyed being 'au naturel' when at sea. There was a beautifully calm sea, few clouds in the sky but fish pots everywhere. I was putting out the line when I immediately had a bite, a smallish barracuda that I put back. Shortly after I caught a large dorado which was soon at the side of the boat but at the last minute he popped the line at the nylon connection, taking the 'barracuda lure' with him. Then another shortly before 18.00, this time he was landed with Else gaffing him, as he was too big for the net. Else took several pictures of me just managing to hold the fish up and of a similar length as myself. It was soon cleaned and the carcass given back to the 'critters' in the sea. It had been eating small sardines. A cold beer and a meal of fresh dorado, a salad and bread and butter was a meal fit for a king! I then took the first watch satisfied with my day and quite replete.

26ᵗʰ April. Have just dropped anchor off St Thomas's Bay off Spanish Town, Virgin Gorda. We entered Francis Drake Channel about 07.00 carefully avoiding the 'Blunders', two rocks barely awash that lie in waiting to rip the bottom out of the unwary vessel. We have sailed overnight from Anguilla. Looking back, we have sailed for eight months leaving Port Penrhyn in Wales for the Scilly Isles, Galicia, Madeira,

Canary Islands, Cape Verdes across to Trinidad, thence to the Windward Islands and the Leeward Islands. Having many adventures and seeing untold wonderful sights, whales, giant turtles, hot and cold waterfalls and undersea volcanoes.

The sail from Anguilla was peaceful in light winds, which unfortunately required the gentle assistance of the old engine to help the sails, ticking over at lowest revs, *clonkerdonkerclonker* – and giving us about four and a half knots. Just enough to ensure that our entry into the rock infested channel was in daylight with the sun behind us, perfect for spotting those sneaky little rocks and coral heads lurking beneath the surface. This area is a graveyard for ships. Off Anagada alone there are over 300 documented wrecks and scarcely three miles away lies the broken carcass of *The Rhone* a 300 foot steamer driven onto rocks by a late hurricane in 1867 and wrecked on Salt Island while attempting to get into deep water during the eye of a hurricane. Then there is a brief lull before the tempest returns from the opposite direction. Most of the crew went down with the vessel that sank instantly.

After shifting anchor once onto a patch of sand - it was holding but hooked under a rock which could have come unstuck. Night sailing however relaxing always seems to require more sleep next day. Lunch was corned beef hash with two eggs which although quite passable did not come up to my own noted hash which has claimed some fame amongst our various crew. The secret is to fry the mixture of fried onions, potato and corned beef until it is brown also adding a touch of curry powder, Lee and Perrins plus dry English mustard. It makes the difference between a meal and a feast!

We then made a round of the other yachts trying to give away the remains of the huge dorado, about 50lbs, that I had caught on the way over. Eventually we gave him to some local lads who bore the tender white fillets away with gratitude. We re-anchored a mile down the coast and had an hour's snorkelling amongst small reefs off the beach.

27ᵗʰ April. Back in the marina to clear Customs. The marina is very tastefully laid out in spacious grounds planted with coconuts and date palms and with fat cows and goats roaming around and pelicans diving amongst the boats for mullet. They hit the water with a resounding splash, surfacing shortly after with a very dazed expression, which does not surprise me. They then sit on the water for a while with their beak partly submerged presumably recovering their wits and breath. Then according to whether the dive was successful they will elevate their beak to allow gravity to assist the luckless fish down the throat or take off for another sortie hoping for better luck.

We took the wee boat down the coast a mile or two to a series of coves formed between piles of gigantic boulders heaved out of the earth in a volcanic explosion. The boulders are often bigger than houses and between them are grottos and canyons dropping down to white sand 30 – 50 feet below. The fish life is prodigious, large vivid blue parrot fish cruising round in stately procession, their protruding teeth specially designed for gnawing the coral with seeming relish. Schools of electric blue angel fish swarm like bees round a particular coral head and black and yellow striped sergeant majors frolic in countless thousands. None seemed unduly bothered by a large mammal in their pale blue domain and one can approach within two or three feet with ease. We went berserk with the camera photographing fish and each other, diving around spectacular stands of elkhorn and staghorn coral or swimming through a sunlit grotto maybe 20 feet down. The whole scene is stunning and as we can now dive with ease down the 30 feet and more it seems totally 3D. Visibility was an amazing 150 feet or so and sometimes it extends to 200 feet. The effect of light and shade and the dappling effect of sunshine is wonderful. Best yet - we visited "The Baths," a subterranean pool roofed by piled boulders between which chunks of light shafted down into the dimness. Round the corner for a final half hour into Spring Bay where a fine fellow of a fish, which we named

Harold, decided to pal up with me and followed me round for half an hour. Whether in stark disbelief at this skinny creature invading his world or in hope of some reward I cannot tell. However, every time I looked round there he was about 3-4lbs of him cocking his googly eyes at me with unconcealed curiosity. Harold was a handsome chap.

We met a couple while sunbathing from Vancouver Island, she being originally from Manchester and he was a Mountie in the R.C.M.P. Both strongly recommending B.C. and Alaska as a cruising ground. Apparently airfares trans-Canada were very cheap. After 4 or 5 hours of incredible snorkelling, as the light was beginning to fade, we returned to the marina for a drink. However, we were lured into taking supper as well, mutton stew with rice and vegetables. The mutton was fine, the rice passable but the least said about the frozen mixed vegetables the better. Back to the boat for a game of Scrabble which after a very close contest, I came up from behind to claim a narrow victory. Whether this was because of or despite a drink that I had at the marina called 'Sex on Virgin Gorda' I don't know. It was advertised as being a surprise you will never forget! It was too! Firstly when it nearly blew my brains out and secondly when I got the bill.

28th April. I fancied a bowl of 'parritch' this morning, until, when pouring the oats into the pan, I noticed they were teeming with life (all cereals stored in sweet jars) only to find that no mites were present but it was heaving with weevils. Ugh! So I resorted to a bowl of muesli, which was subjected to a <u>very</u> close examination indeed. No visitors but tasting slightly less than fresh. After that I felt queasy all morning.

Later we went in the dinghy north of the point to explore Little Dix and Savannah Bay. First as we rounded the reef half a mile off the point a turtle stuck his head up to have a look at us. He was green so we assumed he was a green turtle! Then we came across a tiny unnamed bay on the chart in which we swam 'au naturel' and went ashore in two places, one of which involved wending our way through the seethe and suck of the tide surging amongst the spiky heads of coral. We very carefully returned to the boat and saw a beautiful French angelfish and took several pictures of him or her.

Moving on, we passed Little Dix Bay with over 100 cottages. Nevertheless, the splendid sandy beach over a mile long was practically deserted. Then on round two small headlands into Savannah Bay, sprinkled with reefs, good snorkelling but deserted. We are told that the American recession is hitting the tourist trade hard in the West Indies. Expensive holidays are the first things to go when belts have to be tightened. It must be frightening indeed to have to have spent millions on building an hotel to find it a short time later echoingly empty. On our return to *Ospray* we saw Myrtle the turtle again! The wind had shifted in the night and was now blowing vigorously from the south, which made Thomas Bay a lee shore. During the night we had lost one of our new $50 fenders, which pleased me no end and had hoped to find it on our later expeditions down wind but no luck.

29th April. We went for a walk looking for Spanish Town but failed to find it other than a domestic sprawl. It is very hot and there is aridity about the place, which wicks all the moisture from one's body. One wonders yet again how the islanders make a living. Although many houses are small and mean the folk appear well dressed and well fed to an amazing degree. They are always eating and look healthy with splendid teeth. Only a few generations removed from African slaves brought over in tens of thousands. The different shades of black and marked differences in bone structure from heavy and coarse to exceedingly fine, evidence of the different tribal origins from whence they came.

We were heading for the wilderness area on the south of the island intending to explore this fantastic region of giant boulders, jumbled together and heaped one on top of the other. However, during a call for a cooling drink, I approached a local with a question as to how to get in there. He replied that only the occasional local man had attempted it and it was considered dangerous. Nevertheless, off we went and clambered over several house-sized boulders between each of which grew an impenetrable thicket of spiny vines. Then Else spied an enormous centipede and was decisive in calling an immediate halt to the expedition. So after a halt for fried chicken and rice and ice cream, we repaired to the boat for a brief swim.

30th April. Early this morning while it was still dark, I found a cockroach in my belly button or at least I thought I did. Unable to sleep, I discovered an object round on top and flat underneath. Wide-awake now with nerves a'bristle, I felt for the legs. No legs. Then realisation struck me with a gush of gratitude. It was half a peanut from a snack in bed with a good book last night. Whew!

An overcast day, we were off to a late start and it was after midday when we arrived in the dinghy off 'The Baths' area. A very healthy surge suggested no anchoring and careful snorkelling. Every now and then the rocks would disappear in an explosion of white. Discretion became the better part of valour and back we went past the thundering reefs way offshore where the seas broke over like a cavalry charge of white horses all bearing banners as great columns of white spume were borne back over the waves by the wind. After finding a green coconut we drank the delicious juice with our ham rolls all under the shade of palms.

Back at the boat we donned snorkel and fins. I was first over the side. The first thing I saw on opening my eyes was a largish barracuda watching me balefully from about five feet away, exuding an amazing aura of menace. He swam round in a semi circle then headed directly towards me upon which I lost no time in getting my extremities out of the water. It is no easy task, one that I once thought impossible, to ascend the side of a steel boat wearing flippers. Later we decided he was just taking up his usual position under the boat after being rudely disturbed by my noisy entry. Else thought the whole episode more amusing than I did at the time!

1st May. We had the echo sounder checked by John from *Seven Seas*, who suggested buying a new one. While getting ready for our move across to Beef Island I checked the oil and water levels. The level in the oil sump is very high. I changed the fuel pumps as suggested by John from *Canores*. Then set about changing the oil and discovered five gallons of water in the oil sump, removed it and topped up with oil. I must find out what caused this. We arrived in Beef Island at 17.25. Trellis Bay is horseshoe shaped with a tiny island in the middle. We went to the 'Last Resort' on Bellamys Cay (the island). There was a superb buffet with roast beef, roast pork, chicken, fish, potatoes, rice and salad. Grand entertainment by proprietor, sort of Flanders and Swan style, ultra English songs, ultra English jokes, the Americans were goggle eyed.

Returning all aglow to the dinghy, it was blowing quite hard and on the way back to look for *Ospray* we touched a sandbar and broke the shear pin on the outboard. I took to the oars but could barely make way again due to the increasing wind. Every time we got closer one of the oars would come out of the oarlock and within seconds we were whisked away. Soaked to the skin by now with spray and sweat we clung briefly to another vessel where the skipper, an irate Englishman, declined to invite us aboard. We decided that we would beach the dinghy and sleep under it – by now it was raining hard. We headed towards a motor yacht which had beached itself, was ablaze with lights and rocking on her keel but in soft sand so in no danger.

After appraising the situation and realising that there was nothing we could do, we beached the dinghy and walked up the bay to see if it was possible to drag the dinghy upwind of *Ospray* and come down onto her but we couldn't see her in the rain which was pelting down. Although I thought we should have a cold night wet through under the dinghy, I was prepared for that but was horrified to realise that the whole shoreline, well above high water, was riddled with crab holes and the thought of those crawling all over me with their spiky little feet was loathsome in the extreme. However we decided to call at the beached boat to ensure that help was not required. So we waded through the surf and climbed aboard dripping all over a beautiful Persian rug. Another couple Ian and Mary came over to help and after a committee decision it was decided that the boat was best left 'till morning. Ian took us back to *Ospray* who had turned 180 degrees with the change in wind. We took turns at anchor watch until 05.30 when the wind dropped a little.

2nd May. Slept until 08.30 when Harvey came to take us ashore where we hung about to help if needed while a dive boat came and pulled *Aqua Safari* off the beach, with a little damage to her rudder and prop. She had only just been chartered a few days ago for a fortnight's holiday, which so sadly had come to an abrupt end. Retrieving our dinghy we went back to *Ospray* for a sleep. Then ashore to meet Ian who was interested in hearing about our cruise through the islands. His skipper Geoff was ashore helping someone assemble a triamaran. We helped unload the floats off the trailer then back to our boat where we made ready to entertain Mathew from the tiny 26 foot Virtue *Chinita*. Mathew sailed her from England and we saw him in English Harbour and Nevis, considering him to be the archetypal Englishman. He is still using fuel that he bought in the Canaries of which he carries 20 gallons. Else made a delicious chicken-a-la-queen and a couple of bottles of vino were opened. A grand evening followed which was made none the worse by the fact that Mathew is a Tillman fan. We had many a laugh recounting episodes, especially the one about Eric Shipton who Tillman climbed and adventured with for many years. Always addressing his comrade as Mr Shipton, eventually the exasperated Shipton asked him,

"Why don't you call me Eric?"

"No", replied Tillman without hesitation.

"Why not".

"Because it is such a bloody silly name!"

3rd May. Our friends from the cat came aboard for a chat and a cuppa. Ian's family live on Loch Awe near Dalmally. Ian's mother took up salmon fishing at the age of 64. We have their address and a request to visit them when on our way to or back from Mull. They were considering going down the islands along the route we had followed and were eager to know the best anchorages and the ones to avoid. We related our experiences in Dominica, the whales and hot and cold waterfalls etc.

4th May. Off with a picnic lunch by dinghy to explore 'little Cumanoe' an uninhabited island just a few miles away. We landed on a deserted beach on which we felt like Robinson Crusoe on finding Friday's footprints, when we found a pair of flippers, Else's size! So off we went to explore the local snorkelling Else wearing her 'new' flippers. The main feature of the underwater scene was a huge variety of sea fans, some the most vivid purple and others in a greenish yellow. Some nice crabs, conch shells and plenty of small fish and the odd parrot fish. Meanwhile Else was cruising round wearing her stolen flippers and not long after a large powerboat came into the bay and anchored. A guy jumped out, swimming over to us and saying, *"I say you guys, have you seen a pair of flippers around here?"* "Yes", say I, *"She is wearing them"*. So Else blushing furiously hands them over.

In the scrub on the island, large sleepy lizards were furtively rustling through the undergrowth. Thousands of the poisonous crab apples from the manchineel tree lay in profusion on the ground and impossible to avoid treading on them. So I washed my shoes in the sea as it is said that the juice of these fruit can cause painful blisters. After lunch on our now deserted beach we hauled off the dinghy and shaped our course for long beach on Beef Island where as we came ashore more furtive rustlings betrayed a couple hastily dressing in the bushes. Beaches like this in Europe would be crowded. Back to the ship to light the B-B-Q, and soon we were regaled with the smell of chicken legs roasting.

A satisfying plop announced the opening of one of our specials – cheap bubbly but very good value at £3 a bottle.

5ᵗʰ May. Ian had decided to come with us to Roadtown on Tortola being anxious to sail in as many boats as possible. He is a victim of the recession having had a thriving antique restoration business with 17 employees but the bank pulled the rug and forced him to sell out. So he sold the lot, house, business and all. He is toying with the idea of setting up in the Caribbean. A smart breeze was blowing straight into the harbour. Why do smart breezes always seem to blow where they are not wanted? We had to anchor twice after dragging and two days later we dragged again.

6ᵗʰ May. Up early to do some more jobs and it was as well we were there as there was a knock on the hull and a neighbour in a dinghy telling us that we were dragging and very nearly into another vessel. Scramble and engine on and re-anchored twice but this is poor holding and the wind was very gusty so we arranged to go into the marina at an enormous cost or £20 a day to do our jobs which included cutting a hole just above the water line to augment the cockpit drainage which sometimes works in reverse when someone pumps out the sink – into the same drain.

After a day of doing many long and tedious jobs, all of which went as jobs sometimes do, the opposite way to good, and I won't bore you with the details, we thought we deserved a treat. So we went to the marina for 'happy hour' and stayed on for a meal. Roast duck, all presented with meticulous pro-fessionalism by Antonio. A young lad obviously aiming to rise to great heights in the catering business. We told his boss, the Maitre d', how good we thought he was and Antonio was summoned before us blushing, I imagine, beneath his dusky skin to be complimented. I wish him well.

7ᵗʰ May. I dismantled Mr Samuel No Watts, our wind generator, that's about all he does generate, and gave him a good oiling and lo and behold, he is now going round like a lunatic trying to make up for lost time no doubt. I threatened to throw him overboard. If the wind drops for a moment, he panics and faces every which way frantically searching for the wind. "*Where's it gone, where's it gone? Oh my, oh my,*" I can still only detect the faintest current coming from him. Perhaps he is one of these creatures that have perfected the art of always looking busy without ever actually producing any work.

The Lowerence Depth Sounder is in Cay Electronics for repair but, as usual, the news is not good. I remarked to Else that I should fall flat on my back from astonishment if an electronics engineer ever said "*No problem Sir. Just a little condenser* (or whatever those bits are inside instruments), *which will be $5 please*". Mind you, with labour charges at $50 an hour if it requires more than a wipe with an oily rag, you may as well buy a new one, which I suppose is what it is all about. To rub salt into the wound they all say "*What a beautiful instrument*", gazing at it in rapt admiration. I agree but make the point that I am not interested in putting it on the sideboard but am keen for it to tell me how far away is the bottom of the sea.

9th May. Off to Norman Island where we dropped anchor in 'The Bight' after a sail of 3 to 4 hours in a fresh easterly. We dropped our hook in 25 feet of water and Else went over the side to inspect it and pronounced it almost buried. The bay seems notable for at least two things (which you may wrongly suspect I have in juxtaposition). The noisiness of its goat population and the randiness of its sea birds. The goats spend all their time bleating and shrieking themselves hoarse and the sea birds, a type of black headed gull, seem to be in a constant flurry of mating and incidentally shrieking loudly at the same time, though whether it was the squawk of the female in indignation at yet another assault or the shriek of the male in triumph, I am not quite sure. A large notice on the beach announced that anyone attempting to steal a goat would be heavily fined. Show me the man that would want to, say I!

While yachts were coming in to anchor, a piratical black rig appeared, and went straight through the boats towards the two-master near to the beach. Boom. Powder smoke in the air and the unmistakable smell of gunpowder. They had been fired upon. I jumped not expecting to be in an apparent sea battle with cannon fire. *Galaxy* had been fired upon by *Black Pearl*. One expected to hear a Robert Newtonish voice shout *"Vast firing ye dogs!"*

Needless to say we went in for a snorkel and found a species of fish that we had not seen before. A lovely pair of silvery pink little fish about 5 inches long with beautifully floppy fins. They live in tiny vertical burrows in the sand and on approach of danger they shoot backwards into their burrows tail first then almost immediately peep out shyly to see if it is all clear. There are some very big parrot fish here that are very tame. As you swim past they swivel their eyes at you in mild curiosity as a calf might! We saw several 'Lizard fish', which raise themselves up off the bottom in an aggressive posture showing rows of needle-like teeth.

On the other side of the bay the pelicans were flopping into the water constantly. We went over on the dinghy and found out why. Millions upon millions of silver fish, very much the size and colour of herrings, flashing in the shallows. There must have been tons of them. As we swam out in mask and snorkel, the shoals parted just sufficient for us to pass through and though you could feel the thrum of their bodies as they passed surging within inches of you, never a one could you touch, be you ever so quick at darting a hand out. The pelicans had it all sussed out though and after a few dives sat around in the trees replete. What a life.

The water on the south side of the bay shelved rapidly into about 40 to 50 feet. Boulders and coral amongst which we dived, chasing the fish and trying to photograph a pair of beautiful bronze angelfish. They had no problem in slipping inside the merest slit in the rocks each of which they knew like one knows one's own house.

Back to *Ospray* for coffee and snack, then off in the dinghy to the 'Treasure Caves'. We tied the dinghy to a buoy and slipped over the side into brilliant ultramarine coolness.

Immediately, fish surrounded us, questing like hungry pups. "What have you brought us?" Obviously used to being fed and we had nothing, which would not do for Else at all. So off we went back to the old Barky and heaved the anchor up. In half an hour *Ospray* was moored off the caves and we were in the water with a plastic tub full of mashed sardines and bread. The swarms of fish immediately deserted other snorklers who had bread only and honed in on Else like bees to a hive. Soon Else was invisible behind throngs of fish up to about 5lbs. Mostly yellow jacks and of course it wasn't long before she got her fingers nipped badly and backed off a little to hand me the tub so I should get bitten as well! I gave the rest of the grub away then dived for the bottom at 40 feet still holding the empty tub and hotly pursued by a vast shoal of yellow jacks keen on more sardine. We swam into the caves and I surfaced to find myself looking up a pelican's nostril about three feet away. A few seconds later I jumped as another pelican hit the water about 10 feet away and I could see the stream of bubbles from his dive. I wonder they don't kill themselves as they hit the water with such a wallop. I don't wonder they look so bemused when they surface again. They sit there waggling their heads as if to say *"Strewth, I got that wrong again!"*

This was to be our last snorkel in these beautiful Caribbean waters, at least for the time being, so we made the best of it. It is sensational in every sense of the word. The exquisite caress of the water which is just cold enough to be refreshing and the colour, which varies from the rich ultramarine of an Optrex bottle to the most delectable turquoise. As we get more proficient and can dive with ease to 30 or 40 feet we feel truly three-dimensional in our movements and of course, we have developed a range of hand signals for underwater communication. For example, by means of a few little gestures, *"Oy, come and look at this, but be careful, it looks as if it could be nasty"*.

The brilliant colours and rolling eyes of the fish and all the different colours and shapes of the coral, looking up from 40 feet to see the surface shimmering in the sun and Else's silhouette watching me from above, I shall never forget. The growing feeling of being at home in the water and just the very beginnings of how an otter must feel. Anyone who has seen an otter playing in the water must feel some envy. And so, with a lingering glance into the blue depths where we had spent so many happy hours amongst the undersea canyons and grottos we turned *Ospray's* bows away towards civilization. Back to Road Town to finish odd little jobs and complete the restocking of the vessel for our 870-mile voyage to Bermuda on the way home to England. Goodbye Caribbean. Thanks for having us. See you again sometime.

Chapter 11

Heading for Bermuda
with its infamous Triangle

I contacted the warship *H.M.S. Cornwall* for a weather report and although there was nothing terrible, there was nothing good either. We contacted family to say that we were heading north for our next leg of the voyage. By 14.30 we were out of the marina and heading west to round Tortola. Over the next ten days we headed north. It always took us about three days to get back into the rhythm of being at sea. Else could not stand the sight of coffee and she is usually a coffee drinker only. We found cocoa or hot chocolate the best thing to settle a queasy stomach. It was difficult to sleep with the noise of the engine and when that was off the autohelm could be just as bad. I try to breathe in time with the autopilot, fine for a while until it pauses and I pause, and then I have to take a breath and of course then feel wide awake. I tried sleeping in the fore cabin, which was much less noisy and had success. We had a mixture of squalls, gale force winds and very disturbed seas to generally unsettled weather with fluky winds or no wind at all. Because we are motoring a lot the diesel is disappearing fast.

We both are tired and feel that we could have a lie in. I told Else that when we get back home, I'm going to put a sign on the door, 'Do not disturb', and sleep for a week. The weather looks like it may be changing but the wind continues to come from the north. We make little headway trying the different sails with or without engine. At times we have lovely clear nights, the moon starting to get nibbled at by the mice, lots of stars out casting silver and golden reflections on the sea. We still have the company of a few birds, a tropic bird that visits once or twice a day, the occasional booby and two small black birds with a white band on their tails.

A week after leaving, we put the last 20 gallons of fuel in the tank, about 30 hours left, so we are in need of the wind. '*Please puff out thy cheeks and blow, oh wind!*'

I've just been looking at the flag for Bermuda. 'The Red Ensign with the coat of arms dates from 1915; a red lion holds the wreck of the *Sea Venture*, on which the first settlers arrived in 1609'. The capital is Hamilton and their main industry is based on year-round American tourism. Bermuda is made up of a group of about 300 coral islands.

We both liked doing our daily plot, a pleasure especially on a long trip to see how much closer we are to land. 138 miles to go according to Henry (our navigator) so we may see land tomorrow. I checked our fuel levels that were getting alarmingly low and added some petrol and some kerosene! It amazes me how much we have been able to motor on 'tick over' and with reasonably good effect. I think we use about or just over half a gallon of fuel per hour.

25th May. No sign of land yet, the island is low and the lighthouses can be seen up to 20 and 30 miles away with good visibility. We managed to get a recorded weather forecast yesterday and there is a high-pressure system moving east. I hope we get some more wind, as it is still touch and go getting in under fuel alone, or by sailing slowly, before dark today. It is now 02.45 and we are motoring with the genoa filling nicely, a gentle breeze coming from the south-west, a mild night with moon and stars aplenty. It is now 12.00, land has been in sight for about one hour, just as a gold shimmer on the horizon and then a few glinting specks. Now under main, genoa and engine doing 5 knots, as we need as much speed to get in at daylight.

Time passes slowly when one is anxious about daylight and the amount of fuel left in the tank and the state of the wind. The setting sun was in our eyes so we made out shapes rather than colours to recognise the buoys thereby avoiding the reefs. Soon we had found the narrow channel of Town Cut and were into the bay of St George's Harbour. We 'stood by' to get to the Customs dock while I gave our particulars to the Port Authority. It was a holiday today and we wished each other a good day of what was left. Clearing customs was simple, we were glad not to run out of diesel, there were a few inches left in the tank, the outlet pipe not being at the bottom! The gallon of petrol and kerosene must have just seen us there! The cooking oil was going to be next!

We anchored next to a rusty hulk of a wreck and thought about going into town. It was now dark and we both suddenly felt very tired. A simple meal, a drink or two without ice, then to bed in a safe anchorage after ten lovely days at sea, to be able to sleep the whole night congratulating each other on a safe trip.

St George's is the second oldest English town to be established in the New World. In St. Peter's church there are statues of the King and Queen of Mercia, which were given to the island for the first day of parliament, held in the church. It is the oldest site consecrated for Anglican worship in the Western Hemisphere.

Over the next few days we enquired about mail either at the Harbour Masters or at the Post Office. To receive letters was always a treat. We in turn tried to send post cards or letters so that family and friends could follow our voyage and share in our adventures. Else had to make several trips to a dentist, which was not one of her favourite things to do! We had been to see *The Deliverance II* on Ordinance Island, a full sized replica of one of the two ships built by survivors from the wreckage of the *Sea Venture*. Her barometer was a bladder containing shark oil. If foul weather was forecast, the sediment would rise to the top and its crest would show the wind direction. Here also is the 'Ducking Stool', which on a Wednesday there is a re-enactment for the tourists. "An ancient method of punishment for idle gossipers and slanderers in Bermuda". Cannon can be seen everywhere, certainly an atmosphere of days gone by.

We watched a display of the *Pride of Baltimore* sailing in under full canvas, banners and flags flying, to come to a standstill near to one of the cruise ships. What a sight. We often saw races with a variety of sailing ships eg Looe Luggers coming in with full sails to suddenly about turn, drop their sails and anchor. From one boat in particular, the family would then row ashore and it would be an every day event, as they had no engine. We also met a Scottish policeman, David Kerr, originally from Glasgow, now living in Bermuda for the last 25 years. I was fascinated by his English Bobby's hat and his very un-English shorts!

The official motto of Bermuda is "QUO FATA FERUNT' – "Whither the Fates Lead Us". Their fortunes changing over the years from whaling, salt gathering and ship building initially, to privateering, blockade-runners during the American Civil War, to vegetable growing, Hamilton being known as 'Onion Town', rum-running and now tourism accounts for 70% of their economy.

The buildings are quite different to anything else that we have seen to date. Painted in pastel colours of pink and blue mainly with white sloping roofs and chimneys! The windows have outer louvres, Guyanese style, both for shade and weather protection. All fresh water is from rain collected on the roofs. Initially we could see no guttering but it was cleverly concealed in the roof design.

Some of the place names tickled my fancy. In 'Featherbed Alley' we found an art studio with a 17th century printing press, unfortunately closed. I took a picture of Else stood at the sign of 'Shinbone Alley', that was after deciding not to walk down 'Slippery Hill' where we didn't find the 'Somers Gardens' where the heart and entrails of Sir George Somers lie buried.

While we waited for our next guest to arrive from the UK there were various jobs needing our attention. Hanks to be bought and sewn onto the sails, reinforcing the leech of the better genoa, the fore jib stay to be tightened up, filling up the gas cylinders, laundry and filling the containers of diesel and kerosene. At the dockyard we saw another *Spray* called *Saorsa* and met a lad called Reuben whose boat started coming apart at the seams on the way from USA.

The island is 21 miles long and only Bermudans are allowed to drive cars, hence no car rental shops. There is no illiteracy, unemployment or income tax. Perhaps, this is one reason for everybody being so friendly. We were told that there was to be an open-air concert on the night that Sam was due to arrive. Perfect timing to pick him up at the airport and then enjoy the concert.

We did a bit more exploring of the island by dinghy when we swam, the water getting noticeably colder and then by road. We shared a truckload of diesel with another boat and took onboard about 240 gallons. Else had her last dental appointment and advice on how to deal with her tooth should there be another flare up. We sighted *Chinita* at anchor; Mathew had also taken 10 days to do the trip. One day we set off for 'Eves' bike rental shop. We had hired two scooters, one a two seater, the other a single. Off we went to Hamilton with our speedo registering 0 all of the time, Sam's registering 30 all of the time. We didn't know if we broke the 25 or 35km speed limits. After the chandlers, I bought some English newspapers while Sam and Else went to check on flights out of the Azores for the UK. We visited the botanical gardens, a lovely area in which is the hospital. We saw school children pushing some of the elderly in wheelchairs. Then to a beach for a swim, well, what else might one do on an island when one needs to cool off? Back up on the road a passer-by suddenly stopped and stared at Else. He then started to talk in a foreign language. He was a friend that she knew from Norway who lived next door to her Grandparents. What a surprise! As we did not have to return the bikes first thing in the morning we went to the crystal caves. Two small boys playing cricket in the early 1900's discovered them. A 20-minute tour explained the origins of the stalagmites and stalactites and that it takes approximately 100 years for them to grow one inch.

Chapter 12

Storms, Dragons and Leaping Whales! And that on a Good Day

6ᵗʰ June. There was much strong recommendation from the pundits and the weather atlas to try to get on your way from Bermuda in a certain three-week window. Conditions in this period are usually more favourable although of course not guaranteed.

Yesterday we did the final shop and to get ice. There is a small boat warning 'till 09.00 and quite a few yachts are leaving. Else spoke to Bermuda radio, told them we were going and found that the channel was clear. So anchor up and stowed below decks and we were off. We motored for the first few hours but were soon under sail. Looking at the large chart, the Azores look far away. Sam is feeling ill and looking like a ghost. He stayed below, Else and I taking the watches and self-steering because the autohelm appears not be managing and struggling to hold its course. So a long night with rain, feeling somewhat tired, but sailing well, up to 7.6 knots.

7ᵗʰ June. It is raining; we are manually steering and have done 124 miles on our first day's run. The crew are all feeling out of sorts! The wind is gusting F6-7 but *Ospray* is riding the waves beautifully – we hope that the rigging holds as the sheets are getting a battering. Sam is now helping with the watches and we have decided to do 2 hours on and 4 hours off.

8ᵗʰ June. We woke to a beautiful morning and Herb said that the front should start breaking up today. Whilst in Bermuda we had been given the name of a remarkable man. His name was Herb and his passion was amateur meteorology. Apparently he issues his weather forecast for this particular area and all across the Atlantic. We were destined to follow his very accurate advice for the rest of the voyage. With a change in the weather and sunshine we all felt much better and even managed a proper breakfast of scrambled eggs. I soon had the Cetrek (autopilot) working and think that damp had got into the compass. We had a lazy afternoon but the clouds were building on the horizon so we may have another rainy night in store. Oh well, we should be accustomed to it. Also the roar of a wave coming to get us and then silently slipping under the hull. It's the quiet one sneaking up that gets us down the back of the neck and even up the arms of your waterproofs!

There was stewed chicken for dinner that everyone kept! It ended up being a lovely night, the moon hiding behind some dark clouds so I steered by the stars until they too disappeared. The Cetrek started to say "*Batt. Ala.*" so I will have to check that tomorrow.

9th June. We are gradually starting to eat and drink a bit more and I have managed to fix the Cetrek once more. There was condensation in the face of the compass. Today's run was 82 miles; we have 1503 nautical miles to go to Faial as the osprey flies!

10th June. Sam is reading up about the Azores in the Atlantic Islands guide. The seas are steely grey, spread with flecks of white foam once they have passed under the boat. On the other side, they approach with white horses galloping, no pretty blue to be seen today, directing themselves at the port side. Some making the boat lurch to starboard, playing with her like a small cork in a huge wilderness of water. The ride is still reasonably comfortable despite all I've said. All objects appear to stay below in their ordained places even though they may complain at times making crashing noises.

It is not a nice day, the weather soon worsening to gale force winds. Someone was always on watch in the cockpit with the safety line hooked on. We winged out the genoa and the jib, racing off in the right direction for the Azores, but a dicey rig to keep up at night.

11ᵗʰ June. A very rainy night, the Cetrek complaining again, so he has been covered with a plastic bag. The weather man, Herb, advised those yachts north to go south of east because of the bad weather, gusting up to 30 knots plus. Just why we have been experiencing foul weather! When the wind backed from NW to SW, it also dropped but now the seas still remain quite confused so we are rolling and the water tank is leaking slopping pints of water into the bilges. Oh for a sunny, decently calm and windy day!

About suppertime we crossed the '¼ of the way there' mark which was also 500 miles out of Bermuda. Listening to *Magic Carpet* on the radio, she is 950 miles from Bermuda, averaging 130 miles a day and hopes to do the trip in 14 days. However yesterday, she had waves fill her jib and cockpit so is heading fast for Flores to hide!

12ᵗʰ June. Up at 06.10 with the sunrise, lovely golden colours below floating white clouds, some blue sky but the weather to the south still looks very grey. It's immediately noticeable how much colder the air is, 73 degrees during the night and now it has fallen to 67 degrees. I wonder if there are any icebergs around! I can see shearwaters flying in the air and Portuguese man-o-war flying on the sea.

I eventually got through to Portishead radio and booked a link call. I talked to Kerry and described some of the large waves, she asked *"Were they very frightening?"* Yes, but *Ospray* and her crew were well in control! The genoa has a large tear along the bottom, Else will be busy for a while. I managed to bake bread and scones today, it would seem that few other boats were having baking sessions such as these. Good old *Spray*!

13ᵗʰ June. At sea for one week and a ⅓ of the voyage covered. I've decided that some of the waves like to show off. They come tumbling and growling up to the side of the boat and then dissolve in a cascade of crystal droplets quite silently. I can watch these waves forever, each one being quite different.

On my shift from 18.00 – 20.00, I thought we might be in for some more bad weather. The clouds to the north were lined up like trains while those ahead, in the northeast, were racing towards us across the sun. There seemed a never-ending supply of them. Eventually, it did clear to quite a nice day, 15-20 knots gusting to 25 and the seas gaining in height. So a bouncy ride.

15th June. A pleasant night, no wind, so we continue with the calms (before the storms perhaps) and motoring. It was a beautiful morning and after breakfast Else and I had a lovely bucket shower and shampoo on deck. Time to enjoy the sunshine, taking sun sights and mending the sail. After a deep sleep we listened to Herb and his gale warning not far from us. We are surrounded by lows. Tonight's sky was really quite awesome. About every type of cloud present with huge swirls behind us. We didn't eat much supper expecting a rough night!

16th June. A lovely moonlight night with faint stars and because of the light I could still appreciates the weird clouds all above in the heavens. Full moon was last night. When Else came to wake me for my watch, I suddenly found myself looking at a huge squid. The fishing line was dangling over my head.

We were part of a net that reported in, by radio, to Wendy on *Faydra* daily. Everyone reported in well, suffering the same calms. We have been going south a bit as 35 degrees north seems to be a dividing line for good and bad weather. We are almost half way, S.O.G. 3.9 knots.

17th June. Listening to the 09.30 net, some of the other boats had bad weather like we did last night, are climbing or walking on walls and looking for an aeroplane ticket home. None of us slept much last night. One yacht, we think called *Grand Pesto*, has lost her rudder and has been out of contact for a few days.

The day cleared, a blue patch and some sunshine but still a cloudy horizon and a developing gale forecast for our area! At teatime I was in for a surprise. It was my birthday. Else and Sam produced a cake with candles to blow out, a trifle, my favourite dessert, presents and cards.

The bottle of wine was just chilled; the ice has lasted well, nearly 12 days.

The wind picked up during the night for a good sail doing about 5.6 knots, the moon giving enough light to read the compass. We heard that *Grand Pesto* had her rudder fixed by a passing merchant vessel but there is still a look out for *Ripple* who left the virgin Islands seven weeks ago and has not been heard of since.

18th June. The sky is clearing, huge rollers are coming from the north and we are riding them and heading east. There is a good breeze, we are averaging 4-5 knots.

19th June. Sam and I saw a shark today. We have passed the 45-degree longitude mark and will change the clocks. I have been working on the engine and replaced the solenoid. Else replaced some hanks on the genoa, which with the main is pulling us along nicely in the light winds. The watches have also been put on an hour to coincide with Else's job listening to the radio.

20th June. At sea for two weeks and 698 miles to Faial. We have tried to fish but nothing was biting. Some spotted dolphins came to visit, beautiful and sleek, riding on the bow wave and blowing at us.

After listening in to *Faydra* this morning, Else changed the radio frequency and was able to take part. She spoke to *Moonshine* and *Kirrituck*. She would rejoin *Faydra's* rollcall tomorrow morning. I was very pleased that Else had sorted out our transmitting.

21st June. Listening in to the chat with *Faydra* this morning, three of the other yachts have seen whales. There was also a huge drift net about just waiting to tangle an unsuspecting propeller or two no doubt! Three other yachts are staying with *Nana* who is still taking on water but coping. Someone is trying to fix her rigging and another helping with the engine. He is worried about running the engine and opening up the hole now fixed with epoxy cement. He is a single hander.

It was so hot sewing up on deck earlier that both Else and I had on hats and applied suntan lotion.

Listening in to Herb, it appeared that there is some nasty weather ahead. One boat called *Straight Up* asked about a V.H.F. message that he'd heard? That *Spirit of Iowa*, a square rigger that we saw in St George's, has met with some accident perhaps and that all of the crew were picked up by a freighter? Herb knew nothing of this and would check when he last had contact with them.

22nd June. It is now 04.10, sailing along at 4-5 knots. Recently the wind has dropped at nights causing us to motor. There is a small halo around the moon and the clouds are rushing past heading in a north-easterly direction. There is a low-pressure system moving east and south and a squall line covering a large area moving towards us from the Azores. It is interesting to plot the weather and to see how quickly the systems change. We are very lucky to have contact with someone doing the weather like Herb on *Southbound II* out of Bermuda.

I have just sighted a whale not 20 feet away. After a while another massive spout – I'm sure it is a sperm whale.

The wind has picked up and we are going like the devil, 6-7 knots. During the night it poured and howled. Herb had said to expect the weather to get worse during the night and tomorrow and to be prepared!

23rd June. I woke suddenly during the night; it was Else's watch. The boat seemed to stop when hit by a large wave and did not pick up speed again. Sam and I came up on deck and found that the foot of the genoa had torn. So all on deck and staysail up. Then at 07.00, I woke Sam and Else to help lower the mainsail. We then motored until the genoa had been stitched and could be put back up.

Listening to *Faydra's* net, quite a few boats were having squally weather and *Arcadia,* further north was in 40-45 knot winds. *Destiny* was hove to off Flores because of SE 25 knot winds gusting up to 40 knots. *Geneve* is about 60 miles away from Horta, so everybody is getting nearer to landfall. *Pal* contacted Else for a chat about going into Ireland.

I have looked at our fuel situation and we should have about three days motoring left. The weather will decide whether landfall is Flores or Faial. The latter being 100 miles further away.

Herb warned us not to go north unless we wanted much stronger winds, up to 35 knots and that a boat called *Casandra* hadn't clocked in for two days. There was also a tanker called *Pacific Dawn* drifting about 300 miles away. *Geneve* is now in Horta.

24ᵗʰ June. We had taken the main sail and genoa down expecting bad weather so motor sailed with the staysail.

On the net, *Grand Pesto* was having rudder problems and heading for the rocks off Horta. *Destiny* was still hove to off Horta, *Kirituck* was 37 miles from Flores, *Missy* was adrift with sail problems, *Moonshine* was bare pole in big seas not enjoying life, *Sea Bass* was 55 miles from Horta, *Sunrise* was 6 miles off Flores. Yachts are now rafted five deep in harbour. Later *Destiny* was having rudder problems, a sea anchor out but still broadside to the wind. Both *Moonshine* and *Ospray* offered help 'though we are both behind her. *Moonshine* behind us is having howling winds 30-40 knots and horrendous seas. *Kirituck* contacted us to say that they had passed 15 miles south of Lajes so couldn't report on that anchorage but that the weather was moderating and that would help *Destiny*.

Good news from Herb in the evening, the winds are easing 15-20 knots!

25ᵗʰ June. It is nearly 04.30. The clouds are setting up again hiding the stars but the moon is just managing to shine through a bit, leaving a gold carpet thrown out to us. We all have headaches, possibly due to the noise of the autohelm and engine, the static from the radio or tension from the bad weather and lumpy seas, the boat rolling and lurching. Yesterday's run was 101 miles. At this very moment, there are 178 miles to go and our E.T.A. in Horta is Friday 26ᵗʰ June at 18.21; and hopefully it will be daylight!

We have heard that *Destiny* is about to put up sail and take in her sea anchor having solved her problems.

26th June. We have motored all day to ensure entry at daylight. Ropes, anchor and fenders are at the ready. We had a visit from some dolphins leaping in the air cris-crossing on our bow wave – the common dolphin, with white around their eyes and white bellies.

Moonshine, behind us, is very happy to be closing in, 160 miles away at roll call this morning. Land has been in sight since 15.00, we are now about a mile away on the south coast. All of a sudden we were rounding the breakwater, looking for a berth, the light fading and then some folk came to catch our ropes alongside Palmares, an English, very white, fibreglass yacht! As soon as we were safe and spruced up, we went to find Café Sport, a beer and our post. *Faydra* had been on the V.H.F. to welcome us.

27th June. We found the authorities all in one building so the paper work was soon done. They kept Else's passport as she did not have a visa but she could have it back to get money out of the bank. We strolled up to the marina, looking at the hundreds of ship's logos on the walls. Some very clever and artistic. Beautiful hot showers and white towels were next on the agenda. Then a walk into town to the market, hardware/chandlery shop, post office and to buy bread and one cake using the last of our escudos. I found some more money in another pocket so went back to buy another two cakes only to find that we had left our bread behind, the locals had a good laugh.

In the evening we went to a restaurant with no name, just a sign for eating outside, where we cooked on hot stones (slabs of marble). A lovely evening each of us trying something different, T-bone steak, chicken and pig fish washed down with three bottles of Portuguese red wine. The meal was on Sam – thank you Sam.

28th June. A well deserved lazy morning for all. There is a party this afternoon for all the boat people that crossed from Bermuda to Faial. Everyone is to bring something along so I baked two fruit pies. We had a lovely luncheon at the Club Naval de Horta where we met most of the folk in the net. Laura, from *Missy*, stood up and told a poem about the trip mentioning all the yachts by name and of course mentioned Herb. We also heard about Hugh from *Arcadia* having an anchor and shroud ready for his friend who said that he was going to die at sea. He had even written out the service. That evening back aboard, we sat and chatted about the trip well into the night.

29th June. Sam's made arrangements to leave tomorrow and today has rented a motorbike. Else and I have painted a motif on the marina wall, it depicts an osprey flying, the three names Jim, Else, Sam on the left of the birds feet and on the right, Geoff would be painted in when he arrived.

30th June. Palmares has left and soon the other yacht inside of us will be moving. There is still no room in the marina for us. We saw Sam off, he was sorry to leave the island but not the long passage at sea. He would not volunteer to do a long voyage again; he had been quite sea sick most days and was unable to eat much.

Else went off to do mundane things like laundry while I had the top off the water tank giving it a good clean out. Only the inspection cover had come off causing the water to leak. We went to collect the laundry in the afternoon and relax with a cold beer. Guess whom we met? A very wet looking Mathew, it had also taken them twenty days! Then who should we see at the ferry terminal, Sam, heading for Café Sport to 'phone and say he was delayed by bad weather – the plane never flew.

That night we returned to the restaurant where we cooked on hot stones for a shrimp fondue and chips, salad and deserts and three different bottles of vino verde. Helder, the owner of the restaurant, said he would take us for a trip around the island to see the sights. I shall certainly try to put Horta in an article – wonderful meals, friendliness etc.

1st July. Sam has left again this morning and as the skies are clearer should be able to fly. We exchange information with crew on other boats for onward journeys. Yesterday a small boat arrived from Martinique out of Brazil – a father with his four year old son! Brave!

In the afternoon Helder arrived in his pick up. Off we set Else with our guide in the front and me in the back. A quick stop at his shop for some cushions for me to sit on and a hello to his wife and daughter. After many stops being introduced to friends, tasting passion fruit liqueur and cakes, we were shown the new land formed in 1957-1958, of Capelinos. There had been a volcanic eruption. Nobody died but houses were covered in ash and now lie desolate. We were told that on the day of the eruption there were 500 small earthquakes.

Then through miles of roads, bordered by beautiful green and blue/white hydrangeas, pink and red clusters of roses, yellow and other coloured smaller flowers in the long grasses. At the lower levels the hedges are a mixture of a bamboo/sugarcane looking high grass and these protect the bananas and citrus groves. The hydrangeas were also planted to protect the crops originating at some time from China and Japan. Overlooking Horta, with a view of Pico and the town below, we ducked into a cold tunnel surrounded by tiny colourful flowers and ferns. A short walk and then were suddenly stopped by looking down into a huge crater – the Caldera. The bottom had been a lake until the eruption when it emptied. A lovely afternoon much appreciated.

Later I 'phoned Geoff in Derbyshire and he was able to join us and would be arriving on the 9th.

2nd July. A lazy morning and the sun is shining. Going into town we passed a bare footed man with some cattle. We believe they were being shipped and going for slaughter.

We went to the market, lovely fruit, vegetables, bread, cheese, cakes all sorts. We bought two bags of goodies, met a friend Peter and asked him to join us in a picnic at the nearby park. We were in the shadow of huge trees, the bandstand being repaired, bushes of flowers not unlike poinsettias all around and the splashing of a fountain onto volcanic rocks shaped into a hut, in whose pond swam a regal black swan. Folk were sitting chatting on other benches while children ran, cycled, did handstands against a tree. A mosaic of life and movement and contented happiness!

Our feast was of bolo (a flat bread, sweet and tasting of corn flour), two types of cheese, pears, plums, greengages, very sweet tomatoes and then coconut cup cakes. Peter was a Dutch man that we first met in Bermuda and was having engine problems. His remedy was short and swift *"She broke, so I trow her over de side!"* So that was the end of the matter. It sounded as though that was his general philosophy of life. I was tempted to ask if he was married but thought better of it in case I was given the same reply.

Later at Café Sport we went to the scrimshaw museum. What a treasure, it must be worth a fortune. Beautifully presented and all made in the Azores. Teeth carved with black ink, some coloured, some carved in relief, jewellery, goblets with cups, dominoes, a chess set, ships, sewing implements – all wonderful examples.

4th July. America Day. Off to buy some sausage and home cured bacon that we were told about. I returned to the boat to work on the engine while Else went window-shopping. She saw Mathew and Aubrey on *Chinita* and joined them onboard for a coffee. Later, I found them and went aboard too. They had got a local to scarf together their rudder that had split along the way.

At 16.00 we were invited to visit Paul and Laura on *Pal*. Rudy and Oli were also there, a German couple off *Tandojam*. We are all heading for Cork in Ireland and plan to leave about the same time so were organising a radio net 'NAN' – north Atlantic net. Else would contact Herb for the weather, Rudy would contact the German net and *Pal* would keep us together at 10.00Zulu or GMT – the time zone that we would stick to. We hope to be leaving somewhere around the 12th July.

Leaving there we joined Henry and Martha at the "American" get together and then to Café Sport for supper and a cold beer.

5th July. A lazy day reading and relaxing and chatting to folk as they pass by. Names were being put down on a list for a meal tomorrow night at 'Adego Santa' on ray. Folk are taking along their instruments for a musical evening.

6th July. It's raining but yesterday we collected some driftwood and had our fire blazing which warmed and dried out the boat nicely. I've replaced the autohelm fuse box and Else is doing a food check and general clear up and sorting warmer clothes for the next leg of our voyage.

Soon it was time to meet the others heading for the restaurant for our meal of ray. Sixty of us were sat together. The meal was very tasty; thank goodness Else got the dish with no bones. Who would think that she is of Viking decent! The music was excellent, a mixture of guitars, drums, penny whistles, mouth organs, pacific banjo, violin and a bright and brassy wind instrument.

8th July. We had planned to go island hopping yesterday by ferry but the weather was awful so stayed in and enjoyed a quiet day but still went out in the evening for a beef fondue and a bottle of Dao red wine. Today is cattle day. We have been watching them being weighed and then wedged into containers. Then the vet coming along to inject whatever was needed. We believe they are being shipped to Portugal.

Else is airing carpets etc and I am reading into a tape recorder making a long letter to my Dad describing our last sea voyage and a bit about the island of Faial, the blue island.

We saw a whaling boat being pushed and heaved into a small warehouse so I lent them a hand. Hopefully we can find out more about the whaling on the islands.

9th July. We rented a car in the afternoon so that we could pick Geoff up from the airport and show him round the island. We collected water and took the gas cylinder in to be filled. His flight from Lisbon was late and then we saw him smiling broadly, he had been travelling since 06.00. Then to show Geoff the Caldera, the beautiful fields full of wild flowers as meadows once were. Returning by a different route down tiny cobbled streets and alleys to the boat.

10ᵗʰ July. About midday we set off for a short drive and soon saw an old cart being drawn by two cows yoked together. The wheels were discs of wood, the cart made of cane or wicker and it was carrying young corn shoots. Two straw hatted young boys sat on the back while their father walked behind with a staff. We asked if we could take some pictures.

Soon we had exchanged addresses and were invited to his house. We drove off through the village of Flamengos to the coastal road. Beautiful little houses, flowers, farm animals, racks for drying maize – quite a different life. We returned via the hospital road to see if we could find the farm but no luck. All we saw was a horse, by the side of a wall in the field, with two milk churns lashed one on each side of the animals back. Driving back to town Geoff spied the wagon. We stopped and watched him feed the cattle, and then up he came through a hole in the wall to the field and said, "*please follow*" to his home.

On the way he showed us his horse and promptly jumped on it and galloped off, with only a halter round its head. A fine animal and masterful rider! We were impressed. Then to his house to see his pigeons, his dogs and a sit down with a cold drink and cake. What hospitality. We heard about his family, his work as a printer in America, buying houses and land there and returning here to his land and buying more houses. Quite different from his father and father-in-law who owned nothing. He has ten boys and two girls. One of his sons translated for us, as he still did not speak much English. We said our goodbyes and thank yous and invited him and his son aboard that evening.

We were then busy refuelling the boat – 777 litres of diesel and paid 55555$00! The hose could not reach, so it was all carried and then filled into the tanks. After supper our visitors arrived, Francisco and his son. A lovely chat, trying to learn some more Portuguese, being offered any help and an offer of patatas and tomatas! We said thank you.

At Café Sport later, chatting with friends over a few cervesa, we heard that a few boats have already left. We were planning to go in a couple of day's time. Then back on board, we found a half-hundredweight bag of potatoes, and two carrier bags of tomatoes and corn on the cob. We should have stayed aboard! Else had given them a jar of honey and one of hip and haw jelly. The chef from the yacht next to us came aboard seeing all of these goodies and joined us for a drink and a tomato. The crew take it in turns to sleep aboard; the others are in a hotel! He's a construction worker in New York and wants to own a yacht one day. We went to bed in the wee hours of the morning.

11th July. Rudy was late on the radio and reprimanded by Laura. We meet again tomorrow, same time on SSB 6A. *Pal* will be refuelling tomorrow and then leaving, *Tandojam* wants to do an oil change and refuel but may not stop in Graciosa, as *Pal* and *Ospray* intend to. Geoff and I are working on the engine while Else is on radio watch to catch the weather fax and making a grocery list.

We needed a breather, so Geoff and I went to look at the boats and found Nick Skeetes. He had written about building steel boats in the P.B.O., which I had read avidly, and has him to blame for interesting me to build in steel rather than ferro-cement. We were very pleased to meet each other.

We headed for the market last minute only to find that it was closed with preparations going on for tonight's fiesta; music, dancing and a bar to celebrate Portugal discovering the Azores. We bought some fruit, bolo and a large gallon bottle of wine and headed for the showers. Back at the boat Francisco arrived pleased to see that we were still there bearing more presents and asking for Mr Geoff. He had a large sweet bread, a whole cheese, a bottle of martini, two cold beers for Geoff and me and a juice each for himself and Else. He was vibrant with enthusiasm and talk once again. How do you say thank you to such generosity and kindness? Francisco also said "Next you come, you use my car!"

Armand came over from his boat to ask if they could buy vegetables from him – he would bring potatoes, tomatoes, corn and eggs on Monday evening for them – a price to be arranged upon then. I wonder if he will even charge for them?

That night Else got through to Herb and there is good sailing weather on the way, even if light at first.

Chapter 13

Leaving the Friendly Azoreans for the last Ocean Voyage to Ireland

12th July. Soon after 08.00 we were away from the dock. Saying our goodbyes yesterday to *Moonshine, Pal, Faydra, Janev* and others, taking pictures of the boat paintings and feeling quite sad to be leaving all of these new friends. Long distance sailors are on the whole naturally nice people, easy to get on with, quietly confidant and with quirky personalities. Else got Herb's address so that we could write and thank him in due course.

On the net Rudy was late again. Else relayed the weather and got voted 'President' by Laura. Rudy will be leaving tomorrow direct for Falmouth.

On the way across the shout of 'whales' went up! A large male, a mother with two young and several immature, whom we thought might be pilot whales. We also saw a few turtles, one the size of my palm, paddling by.

We tried our hand at fishing but no luck so headed for the breakwater in Praia. Men stood and watched us, no offer of help until the Guarda came to help. Then they took our ropes, as it would have been difficult for us to climb up the tyres onto the high wall.

That evening while we ate aboard, streams of cars were stopping to look at the boat – we don't think many yachts visit the island – we are an interesting novelty!

Tandojam has left and is not far from us and like *Mambo* is having very little wind. *Khaula* has left and on her way to Ireland.

13th July. We were up early to get the bus at 09.00 but it never came. Chatting to the policeman he advised us to thumb for a lift. So we walked and walked, a tractor, a motorbike, a truck and then we got a lift on a minibus type vehicle into Santa Cruz. We had walked almost halfway. Then to find the bank. I was called into a small room. Else was called into the same small room. Their machine had broken my card. Eventually Lisbon said 'yes' to giving me some money and with huge apologies they returned my card well sellotaped.

Along the coast road to the harbour, we went into a museum with a whaleboat, built in 1954 and last used in the 1970's. We saw all of the implements used, parts of the whale showing a jawbone and how huge the teeth must have been; Else could fit her fist into the gap left by a tooth. I also took a picture of her sitting in the boat. The harbour itself was very snug, not much room for a fishing boat let alone anything bigger. As we explored we passed a large open room where women were doing their washing. It looked like a communal laundry, the women enjoying themselves and having a good old natter. Next door to which was a field, and on that field was a young man ploughing with a horse. Now I have kept and bred horses for many years, both Shire horses and more latterly Welsh cobs. This was most interesting to watch. He ploughed a good line and certainly had a wonderful manner with the horse. We waved a good bye and headed for lunch and to find a taxi back to the boat.

The taxi driver dropped us at the boat to offload our groceries and then for a drive. We were slowly following a herd of cattle when we noticed a small house on the left with an elderly man tending a fire against the side of the house, over which sausages were hung and being smoked. A walled garden protected a stand of maize plants. Then through a tunnel and into and down the volcano. We parked and walked down stairs and more winding stairs until we stopped to pay a fee and down we kept going round and round into a huge cavern, large flat surfaces on the ceiling. I would hate to be around in a rock fall. It was huge, no 'mites' and only very small 'tites'. Lights lit up the walls;

there was one sulphur fumerole and a large lake. Quite spooky. Then back up 180 steps, a few earth steps and to the car, hearts thumping. Geoff had taken some video from each window on the way up which should be quite effective. We then drove around the caldera and up to the church that we could see from the boat when lit up at night.

Geoff and I are fishing and there is a good breeze out at sea. Soon it will be time to go to 'Toma do-la-la' for burger and chips, as we believe it is the only food served in the town. Else telephoned her sister to say we will be sailing tomorrow. There was a good weather report from Herb even though the winds will be light initially and the sky overcast. We have to watch out for a gale system near Nova Scotia. It will be our last whole night's sleep for a while; I remarked how well we had managed for the last eleven months.

14th July. We cleared out with the Guarda. I was worried, as we had no papers to say that we had arrived or left the island. I went to find the diesel pumps only to find that the man who sold it was to be found in the tobacco factory

Francesco and sons going to feed the cattle, Azores.

Waiting patiently.

Francesco showing his horsemanship.

Ospray's logo at Faial marina, Horta.

opposite. Geoff and I both rang England to say we would be leaving for Ireland today.

Else was late for the 10.00 'NAN' net – and apologised. *Pal* is refuelling and possibly leaving tomorrow depending on the weather. We were away by 11.00, motor-sailing with a light SW, the occasional large swell behind us. Else put Cork, as a waypoint, into Henry – 1124 nautical miles to go at 041 degrees, ETA possibly 22nd July. Not a bad days sail and we are soon back into a routine. At 23.30 the radio transmission was reasonably good, the weather remaining the same, Herb thanked Else for a good report.

15th July. At sea again. We are doing two hours on and four hours off, myself, Else and then Geoff. So Else has the pleasure of waking Geoff, not always an easy job, he sleeps deeply and when woken always jumps making Else jump! It was rare to see Geoff in a bad mood, but when he was woken first thing in the morning that would usually be one of those few occasions. The awakener would give a quick

Whaling boat on Graciosa.

shake and step back two paces, much like one would do with a sleeping tiger. Wakers beware! This went back a long time to our camping days as youths.

Pal will be leaving Horta today and trying to catch up with us while we are catching up with *Tandojam*. Else is plotting a chart with all of the boats, progressing daily. Herb has given good weather for the next 24-36 hours but then we have to watch these lows again.

16ᵗʰ July. The moon is out every so often, a rogue large wave catching *Ospray* off guard and sending us rocking from side to side. At 11.00 yesterday we had 999 miles to go and the days run by GPS was 125 miles, not bad.

We managed to sail most of the day, once mistaking a ten-foot long log encrusted with barnacles for a whale. A while later we passed a radar reflector on top of a buoy along with a red buoy. I thought of stopping to examine it but that would mean putting the engine on, changing the sails and perhaps there would be a line attached somewhere waiting to catch our propeller. It is amazing how many things go floating by so close to the boat.

Else chatted with quite a few people this morning – Rudy is well ahead, *Pal* motoring with no wind, *Cava* is reefed in as they are much further north and *Kirituck* is doing well. *Moonshine* said hello from Horta, most of the crowd are now moving out. Else was asked to call *Picolo* on VHF who left yesterday. *Nightwind* might join us tomorrow on 'NAN'.

Talking to Herb at midnight, he said our course was OK; we are now north of his line and should be getting 15-20 knot winds from the west. *Pal* was advised to head for our position and *Cava* was warned that they are very close to heavy winds.

17ᵗʰ July. Yesterday's run was 107 miles, ETA approximately one week. We are having a nice day but *Pal* has fog and *Whitehound* a bit behind her has limited visibility. *Mambo* should be in sight of land this evening.

We had the old genoa down to do some sewing and I spied something by the bow. Two whales slowly swimming past us. Very little of their bodies were above the water, there was a short bushy blow and a small hump on their backs.

While supper was being made there was a sweet smell that could not be identified. I went down to check the batteries in the engine room and found one of the leads sparking against a can of oil, which by now had a hole in it. Another look around and Geoff found a tin of black hull paint had spilled. What a strong smell, hope we sleep safely in the aft cabin tonight.

Our run today is 102 miles and we are heading east. Else's plotting of the various boat's positions shows well where everybody is in such a large ocean.

18th July. It had been a dark, wet night and the fumes in the cabin unpleasant, so we left one of the boards in the doorway to the main cabin from the cockpit out. I woke Geoff and Else shouting *"Whale!"* There were three of them, huge, larger than *Ospray* and right behind us. I could see the white underside of its head, dark grey backs, blowing, a double blowhole, and then rolling on into the water showing a sickle shaped dorsal fin. Often they would roll onto their side showing a light, perhaps white, belly and sharply defined edges of a fluke. The book says – *"tall blow (4-6m height) shaped like an inverted cone, followed by long shallow roll showing fin"*. The Balaenoptera Physalus, or Fin Whale, is 18.0 - 25.0m (slightly larger in females) weight circa 80 tons. They were certainly a lot larger than *Ospray* who was 40 foot long and weighed 17 ton. They stayed with us for a least half an hour, on either side, diving on the stern, turning slightly so that we could see an enquiring eye watching us while it smoothly descended and surfaced again at the bow – quite awesome! So close at times, that we were sure to hold onto the boom and gallows in case the vessel was nudged accidentally. A nudge from a beast weighing 80 tons is some nudge! Else commented that her feet in wellies would just fit their blowhole. And of course, no one had a camera or video machine to hand and we did not want to leave this majestic scene to go below. Two of them tended to swim together, the other showing off on his own. We could see the white patches on the whales' head about 30-40 feet away. They feed on plankton, fish and squid, their diet varying with the seasons.

Of course, Else had to tell the net about the whales! Rudy said that he had a similar incident with one whale that got too close, so put the engine on and off went the whale. *Whitehound* has had her mainsail tear from luff to leech but can sail on with the sail fully reefed. *Pal* is catching up south of us and *Kirituck* hope to be in La Coruna tomorrow morning. *Cava* is staying south at 48 degrees because of the stormy weather north of 50 degrees.

It was the end of the bolo so I baked a lovely batch of fresh bread. Nothing like the smell of fresh bread. Herb, tonight, said that the weather was generally clearing.

19th July. There are some large waves trying to keep the cockpit washed clean. It is a reasonably warm day with sunshine. I spoke to my brother Mike in England and Geoff spoke to his wife Joyce; Else spoke to her brother Stuart in Trinidad so everyone knew we were safe and well. Mike and Mary want to meet us in Kinsale.

20th July. We are racing along in the gusting winds, at 6 knots, our course is 050 degrees. The sun is rising and it is time for Else to wake Geoff. Geoff says that Else enjoys it, especially when she comes in dripping wet, with a smile on her face saying that it is a bit wet outside!

Else overslept and was late for the net. Laura thought something terrible had happened. Perhaps with an amorous whale! We did see a few huge spouts on the horizon but nothing more, perhaps because we had the engine on most of the day and raced along at 6-7 knots. Else is writing to her family in Trinidad and has put her address as 'nearing the Porcupine Abyssal Plain', which is adjacent to the Irish continental margin and is between 4000 and 4850 m deep. Which I would have thought is a little too deep for porcupines!

21st July. Herb says that there are higher winds on the way, 25-30 knots, but today will be light winds and possibly cloud. Else relayed *Pal's* position last night and will again tonight. They can hear but have difficulty being heard.

Listening to the net today, we are now further north than *Tandojam* but they are further east. Rudy left their water maker on last night and this morning found the boat full of water. Now it's *"guess what we are having for dinner?"* Cans with no labels! *Galatea's* sails are fixed now but their autopilot has stopped working. Paul on *Pal* also said their autopilot wasn't working for the last few days. *Pal* and *Whitehound* can just see each other. *Pal* has decided to follow us into Kinsale. Then, bang, our steering cable broke, so that took a good hour to fix. Some diesel overflowed but hopefully not into the water tank.

Else gave me a haircut and a beard trim – she was having no wear worn sailor arriving in Kinsale! She commented how well and relaxed I looked.

We have done our best day's run -136 miles, motor sailing all of the time. In the afternoon I saw a whale breech twice with a colossal splash so we altered course and saw it blow often, then dive, flukes in the air and that was that. So instead of heading NW we headed NE again. During the afternoon we heard several explosions, once when there were dark clouds about and the second time with fair weather. There were no ships on the horizon and no planes above, a mystery.

22nd July. A pleasant day but then a very rainy night, winds blowing to 30 knots or more. Herb was a bit worried about us staying in the front and suggested going west. We decided to do more northing for a while then back to NE. By 07.00 the weather had cleared and we had sailed well through the night on the genoa.

23rd July. Geoff was the first to see land, about midday, just visible as a hazy lump beneath the tell tale cloud cover. By 16.00 Fastnet rock and lighthouse were clearly visible, we were all quite excited, shall we go into Baltimore or continue sailing up the coast to Kinsale? Else tried to tell Herb that we were nearly at Kinsale but the reception was terrible. The evening was, however, lovely, the moon coming up and looking like a slice of orange reminding me of a sail, lit up from below in front of us. The Kinsale lighthouse was just behind the moon. We needed to keep our eyes peeled for the fishing boats going past. Else again tried to thank Herb for getting us across the ocean safely. She hopes that he heard our transmission. We certainly appreciated his interest in us!

24th July. Geoff and I were fishing off the Old Head of Kinsale. I shouted below to Else *"Get the net, quick"*. I had a large cod on the line and needed help. We had already caught a few mackerel and as there was no hurry to get into harbour, we were drifting half a mile from the land and enjoying the peace and quiet. It was a beautiful morning, a beautiful day and we were three very happy people. About 10.00 we stopped fishing, Else had readied the boat for going in, sails down etc, Geoff and I got the anchor up and readied for use if necessary.

On the way in Else noticed two figures on the hillside waving, it was Mike and Mary welcoming us! They were at the marina ready to help us tie up alongside Donald's boat. A drink of whisky from Donald and then we opened two bottles of champagne. All of this after one slice of toast! We had arrived and tied up by 11.45 Zulu. A lovely homecoming to Ireland. I showed everybody how fit I felt and pulled myself up the shrouds like a monkey up a coconut tree. My brother Mike said *"The bugger's done it"*, we were both smiling broadly like Cheshire cats.

We needed food and a strong coffee, so went our separate ways. Mike had booked a table at 'Bernards', the best seafood restaurant in town. And it was excellent. Back on board we finished off an excellent day with a wee dram and then to bed.

25th July. Awakening at 09.00, we found *Whitehound* rafted in front of us. Mike and Mary arrived while we were breakfasting on fresh mackerel fried in butter and covered in oatmeal. They have set off towards Bantry Bay in their rented car. I think we wanted to stay quietly, perhaps a nose about town and to welcome *Pal* on their arrival. About 13.00 they came up on the VHF and anchored nearby. We would see them later and had kept a bottle of champagne for their arrival.

That evening, after dinner, when Mike and Mary had returned we spent an excellent evening listening to accordions, banjos, guitars, singing and dancing in a nearby pub. Our feet tapped all the way home to *Ospray*.

26th July. Mike and Mary joined us for lunch on the boat looking at the photograph albums of far-flung places. Soon they were away driving to Dublin for their return flight. Then we spotted Paul and Laura rowing ashore. They had slept round the clock as without a working autohelm they had been steering the boat for the last eight days. We opened our last bottle of champagne and also shared it with the crew of *Whitehound*, celebrating our safe arrival in Ireland. That evening whilst I was cooking our supper of mackerel, the lady on the boat outside of us said, *"what a delicious smell"*. My answer was, *"would you like some fish?"* We gave them some cod and ling as we still have so much from our morning fishing the day we arrived. Later we went to find some live music, which we had enjoyed enormously the night before. We were not really looking for the Guiness or Murphies!

27th July. The day was spent doing a bit of shopping, Else was able to get duty free items as she has a Trinidad and Tobago passport, and a lovely walk along the river Bandon to the west of Kinsale. In the bright sunshine we could see the purple patches of heather for miles on the hillsides. Else picked some heather and wild flowers for the boat, a nice feminine touch while we are alongside.

Shall we eat aboard or ashore? We looked at menus and for live music and found it at the same place '1601'. Crab salad for starters, Geoff and I had Irish stew while Else had a steak. There was no room for dessert. The music was good, Irish drum (baron), guitars and banjo. Two couples joined our table who amused Geoff and I all night with their lack of any expression. They only moved their lips while drinking! They reminded me of a radio programme – the Glums or something like that.

Geoff back in Ireland.

Safely in an Irish Harbour

Back on the boat we had a nightcap, the malt is now finished. Else left us talking into the wee hours of the morning. I had bought Geoff a present of a tot glass, which had to be christened!

28ᵗʰ July. Else was up first, not surprisingly, having a leisurely coffee on deck and watching the world go by. Paul and Laura came by while Else and I were reading and listening to music, Geoff was still asleep. We said our goodbyes.

Soon after midday we had cast off the ropes and were leaving the marina. Many boats had already left and it was starting to look quite empty. The winds were very light so we motored along the coast, stopping to fish where there might be a likelihood of a good catch. Lots of mackerel but I was looking for some monkfish. By 17.25 we were alongside a trawler in Ballycotton. Their engine was running and we were told they would be leaving in a few minutes. Two hours later, we switched off our engine, no signs of departure next-door. By this time three other yachts were alongside of us, one out of Dungarvan. There was very little room left in the harbour. It was choc-a-bloc with large trawlers against the south facing wall, a lifeboat moored in the centre of the harbour and smaller fishing craft dotted all about inside. Both walls were teeming with men and boys fishing, cars coming and going and folk stopping to see so many foreign boats. While we waited and had a fish dinner, I had a sleep and Geoff and Else played a game of Scrabble.

Then at last someone came from the trawler saying that the men were in the pub having a drink. They had been there drinking for the last five days since coming ashore! We went up to the pub for a drink and met them, all with eyes half open and very chatty. We were told not to worry; they would just *"shlip out from under yer and yer won't feel a ting!"* We made sure to be on *Ospray* when they were leaving, not wanting them to slip our lines and find that our raft of boats were up on the beach somewhere next morning. So we waited.

About 00.30 they arrived, slipped out forwards to lie in the harbour entrance and leave early morning from there.

One of the men kept asking, *"have yer got any of that there contraband?"*

29ᵗʰ July. We went ashore in Ballycotton to stretch our legs, went down to the shore where there was a bird sanctuary, saw pretty houses and gardens, folk were friendly and there were wild hedges full of blackberries which we munched on. At noon we left, now heading for Dungarvan, Else cooking lunch of white pudding (recently bought ashore), egg, bacon and mushrooms with soda bread. Again we motored and fished and read and relaxed and enjoyed life!

The entrance to Dungarvan looked a bit tricky trying to make out the markers, however we managed and a fisherman in a small boat showed us where to go alongside. Again loads of people came to chat. *"Where had we come from?"* *"How long at sea?"* All about *Ospray*. One man asked for an interview and to take some photographs for the Dungarvan Observer, his name was Tom Keith. We will be in the section – 'In Town This Week' – and he had promised to send us two copies, one for me and one for Geoff. I lent him the BWee in-flight magazine with my article on Joshua's Journey, which he will return, with the newspaper article.

When he left we had our supper of fresh mackerel, caught that afternoon, bread and butter with the last pickled cucumber and tomatoes from the Azores.

30ᵗʰ July. We were up early to avoid the low tide; it was already ebbing fast with seaweed and other flotsam and jetsam streaming past. People are so kind. Yesterday, we had offers to go and fetch diesel, we met a Dutchman who had come for the fishing for over forty years and we met the son whose father's boat had come from Dungarvan and who helped to tie us up when the trawler moved out. Many of these folk were on the dock to wish us farewell. I just managed to turn *Ospray* in the space between the wall and fishing boats and the strong tide soon had us heading for the open bay with its large bird population and amusing cormorants. While we were in Ballycotton, we had watched a cormorant fishing, quacking and chuckling to himself or herself, diving then coming up with an eel or a fish, washing it down with water and a lovely wag of the tail. It's head like a periscope, zooming left and right for traffic or people getting too close, diving and coming up in a different place from the direction you thought he was diving towards – cunning bird!

So we are now making for Dunmore East. These harbours along Ireland's southern coast have been haunts of ours for many a summer sailing holiday in the past. June or September was usually chosen to avoid the school holidays. Ireland was always a favourite for good sailing, safe anchorages just a short sail away from each other and in the evenings a good meal with live music. The quality of the craic is exceptional and found nowhere else in the world. Once while I was at the bar ordering a couple of Murphies, I fell into conversation with a local who chatted away to me for a good twenty minutes while Else waited. I quite failed to understand anything he said and hope that I nodded or shook my head at the appropriate times!

A terrible thing has happened to Else, we have run out of coffee! And she is the purser! It is nice and warm on deck, even for sunbathing. How shall we adapt to life based on land again? I suppose quite easily!

By 16.00 we were tied alongside a trawler and walking up to town to get coffee, bread etc. We found peat reasonably priced so would get that on our way back. Back aboard, *Four Quarters* came alongside, another yacht who is Irish, the skipper from Liverpool.

31st July. I decided that we needed to be off early and the trawler inside of us also wanted to leave. Else wanted a few things from the local shop and one of the crew threw her his car keys, as she wanted to get the peat. Else asked, *"which side of the road do you drive on here?"* We have driven in so many countries that she was a bit confused. After a deep pause for thought the answer was, *"Oi tink it's on der right!*" Else spent all of her change and put the last £1 coin into the R.N.L.I. boat moneybox. We picked up a bucket of ice, Geoff finished filling up with diesel, all aboard and ready for the off.

We motored and fished and then the shout went up of "whales" once more. Orca, killer whales, when we least expected to see them. I could see a large male blowing with a huge triangular dorsal fin standing upright out of the water, also females with more sickle shaped dorsal fins and it looked like young whales close alongside their mothers. They were quite definitely in hunting mode. The whole pod zigzagged through the water keeping an accurate formation, the same distance apart. I felt a shudder at the sheer orderliness of this hunting pack and felt mighty glad that they were not hunting me!

1ˢᵗ August. We are back onto the watch system, doing odd jobs, fishing, sleeping and making sure that we have *Ospray* looking shipshape on arrival. A cold night for the last one at sea, thunder and lightening, rain, fog, the lot! We made a very fast passage across St George's Channel to Wales. Visibility was poor going over the sand bar, the entrance to the Menai Straits and we could just make out the channel markers. We were coming in with the tide and were bombing past the mussel bank markers at well over 10 knots. Else had lit the fire hoping to warm up the cabin but it smoked horribly. And it was time to wake Geoff to help with this tricky bit of navigation through the Swellies to Port Penrhyn. Poor Geoff woke and sat there gasping while Else laughed and tried to explain. He thought the boat was on fire but wasn't doing anything about it! Else was crying tears and dripping wet standing in a fug of smoke. As soon as I had turned the chimney pot all cleared and there was soon a warm cosy cabin below compared with the wet watery 'dreich' day breaking above.

At Port Dinorwik, there were waves from shore, Joyce, Margaret, Bernard and Mave. We were also sailing through a regatta with a few close calls as boats were tacking while racing, others coming towards us and *Ospray* trying to find her way in enough water. There was a wave from one of the moored boats, it was Robin, onboard his yacht, who had taught Else at night school while doing her Day Skipper course. Next, in the distance approaching us was a brown hull with two masts, our old friends, Nigel, Di and the children, blowing horns and ringing bells! We had put all of our flags up for the occasion and were being escorted to Port Penrhyn. Geoff jumped aboard Nigel's boat and filmed us and then when going alongside. Bernard was there to take the bow rope while Else jumped ashore with the stern rope. I was happy to have brought us safely into our next and final port safely but most of all my special thanks to my beloved *Ospray* who had looked after us so well on the high seas for the last year! It was midday.

Joyce had brought a bottle of champagne, wine and food. We all had a great time chatting and laughing. About 14.00 my son Rob and my Ex Ruth arrived with a lovely almond cake, soon to be devoured by all, especially the children. Unfortunately she had not brought Ginnie, Else's terrier. She would have to wait to see her.

Goodbye to Geoff, he had been great company and a very competent crewmember since the Azores. Else had telephoned Customs in Holyhead and then Immigration in Liverpool. All we have to do is to post the original form that we had been given on departure. Else queried the fact that her passport had not been stamped but was assured that all was in order.

Rob and Ruth took us out for an Indian meal in Bangor and when back on the boat Nigel and Di joined us for a drink, the bottle of sparkling wine that Ruth had brought. Getting on towards midnight we were starting to droop visibly and were left to fall into bed, safely moored back in our old berth against the wall. Two green eyes staring out of the darkness on the shelf reminded me that we had a visit from next door's cat. I was overcome by a peculiar feeling; I had no plans of where to go next, nice but unsettling.

Reflecting on the voyage and the performance of our *Spray,* we had sailed ten thousand miles in comfort and safety with gales up to F10. I can honestly say, there was never a time when we felt our little ship *Ospray* was in danger! Apparently, on the run from Bermuda to the Azores, only two out of fourteen boats came through without damage. Well done *Ospray* and thanks for a wonderful trip!

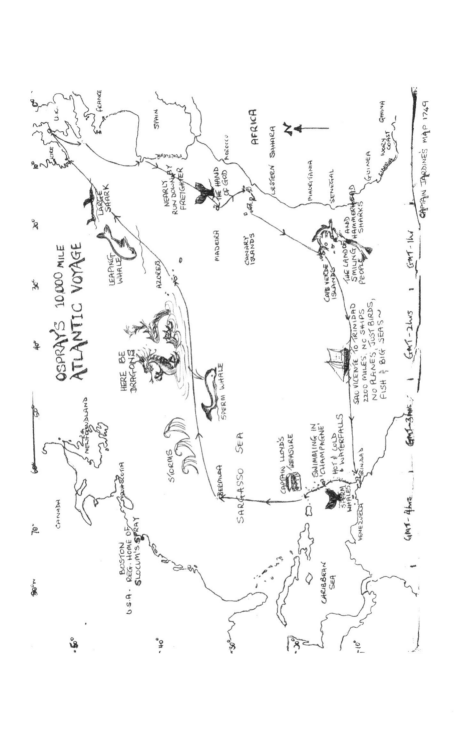

Brief Description of Book

A QUIET DAWDLE AROUND THE ATLANTIC!

The author describes building his boat in steel with his son Rob, a welder, together developing and perfecting many new techniques and methods, from Bruce Robert's plans of Slocum's *Spray*. Choosing, felling, treating timber for masts and interior fittings; sourcing materials for ballast and arranging transport to the sea over eighty miles away.

After shakedown voyages to the Hebrides he met his wife Else and together they embarked on a yearlong 10,000-mile voyage, full of incredible sights and sailing adventures. Snorkelling in the warm Caribbean amongst vast shoals of multi-coloured fish and many close encounters with 80-foot whales!

About the Author

James Mellor was born in Buxton, Derbyshire, where he was educated and worked as a chemist/biologist in Stockport. His first address as a married man, not one for a social climber, was No. 1 Gas Works Cottages, Buxton, lying snugly between the Sewage Treatment Works and the Gas Works. It was sometimes said, "that it was a good wind that blew no ill!" He then moved to Shropshire as assistant manager and chemist for what later became Severn Trent Water Authority. He was promoted to Manager and moved into the farmhouse.

He had read Slocum's book "Sailing Alone Around The World" and was vastly inspired by his adventures and his huge regard for the *Spray*. One of the reasons he decided to build a copy of the *Spray* in steel was the fact that his eldest son was a welder, a good one, and could teach him the basics. As the large barn became redundant, he was allowed to utilise this space, in which to build his boat, for a peppercorn rent.

Hundreds of hours spent reading and researching, always using many, rather than one option, for methods or materials. And three and a half years later *Ospray* was born, in Shrewsbury, eighty miles from the sea. Due to lack of depth in his pocket, he decided from the start to make whatever fittings could be made and if possible use local spruce for masts and local exotic hardwoods such as laburnum, holly and damson for fitting out the interior of the vessel. Boat Jumbles were avidly searched for all manner of fixtures and fittings e.g. anchors, chains, winches, a lovely old set of deadeyes (made from lignum vitae), charts, compass and wooden pulley blocks to name but a few!

Ospray was launched in 1983 in Port Penrhyn, near Bangor and after several years of shakedown cruises with family and friends to Ireland and Scotland (unfortunately

Rob suffered badly from *mal-de-mer* so could not join the boat). Plans were being made to voyage south with his new partner Else, a Trinidadian. *Ospray* left her berth for a yearlong voyage south to Trinidad, calling at Galicia, Madeira, the Canary Islands and Sao Vicente in the Cape Verdes, then up the Caribbean chain of islands and back to the UK, via Bermuda, the Azores and Ireland. They returned after a 10,000-mile voyage, with the feeling that they could easily continue with seaboard life. They met many couples, which had sold their houses to buy a boat and had spent several years cruising the balmy Caribbean at little cost. Jim and Else worked out that their year's expenditure was well under £10,000 without stinting!!

The author and his wife cruised on *Ospray* to explore the Argyll coast and eventually found a delightful island called Seil where they still live with their three Springer Spaniels. *Ospray* was sold some time ago and Jim and Else would like to know of her present whereabouts and experiences.

Lightning Source UK Ltd.
Milton Keynes UK
UKOW06f0622061013

218540UK00010B/16/P

9 781781 488102